Adele

Other books in the People in the News series:

Maya Angelou
Glenn Beck
David Beckham
Beyoncé
Sandra Bullock
Fidel Castro
Kelly Clarkson
Hillary Clinton
Stephen Colbert
Suzanne Collins
Miley Cyrus
Ellen Degeneres
Johnny Depp
Zac Efron
Eminem
Roger Federer
50 Cent
Glee Cast and Creators
Jeff Gordon
Al Gore
Tony Hawk
Salma Hayek
Jennifer Hudson
LeBron James
Jay-Z
Derek Jeter
Steve Jobs
Dwayne Johnson
Angelina Jolie
Jonas Brothers
Elena Kagan
Alicia Keys
Kim Jong Il
Coretta Scott King

Ashton Kutcher
Taylor Lautner
Jennifer Lopez
Tobey Maguire
Eli Manning
John McCain
Stephenie Meyer
Barack Obama
Michelle Obama
Apolo Anton Ohno
Danica Patrick
Nancy Pelosi
Katy Perry
Tyler Perry
David Petraeus
Queen Latifah
Daniel Radcliffe
Condoleezza Rice
Rihanna
Alex Rodriguez
Derrick Rose
J.K. Rowling
Shakira
Tupac Shakur
Will Smith
Gwen Stefani
Ben Stiller
Hilary Swank
Taylor Swift
Justin Timberlake
Usher
Serena Williams
Oprah Winfrey

Adele

By Katherine Krohn

LUCENT BOOKS
A part of Gale, Cengage Learning

GALE
CENGAGE Learning

Detroit • New York • San Francisco • New Haven, Conn • Waterville, Maine • London

Library of Congress Cataloging-in-Publication Data

Krohn, Katherine E.
    Adele / by Katherine Krohn.
        p. cm. -- (People in the news)
    Includes bibliographical references and index.
    ISBN 978-1-4205-0882-6 (hardcover)
    1. Adele, 1988---Juvenile literature. 2. Singers--England--Biography--Juvenile
literature. I. Title.
    ML3930.A165K76 2013
        782.42164092--dc23
        [B]

                                                          2012038767

Lucent Books
27500 Drake Rd
Farmington Hills MI 48331

ISBN-13: 978-1-4205-0882-6
ISBN-10: 1-4205-0882-2

Printed in the United States of America
1 2 3 4 5 6 7 17 16 15 14 13

Contents

Foreword   6

Introduction   8
A Regular London Girl

Chapter 1   12
A Gifted Child

Chapter 2   23
Discovered!

Chapter 3   35
The Making of a Star

Chapter 4   46
More Heartbreak, More Hits

Chapter 5   66
Career Crisis

Chapter 6   78
Getting Real with Adele

Notes   89

Important Dates   96

For More Information   98

Index   100

Picture Credits   104

About the Author   104

Fame and celebrity are alluring. People are drawn to those who walk in fame's spotlight, whether they are known for great accomplishments or for notorious deeds. The lives of the famous pique public interest and attract attention, perhaps because their experiences seem in some ways so different from, yet in other ways so similar to, our own.

Newspapers, magazines, and television regularly capitalize on this fascination with celebrity by running profiles of famous people. For example, television programs such as *Entertainment Tonight* devote all their programming to stories about entertainment and entertainers. Magazines such as *People* fill their pages with stories of the private lives of famous people. Even newspapers, newsmagazines, and television news frequently delve into the lives of well-known personalities. Despite the number of articles and programs, few provide more than a superficial glimpse at their subjects.

Lucent's People in the News series offers young readers a deeper look into the lives of today's newsmakers, the influences that have shaped them, and the impact they have had in their fields of endeavor and on other people's lives. The subjects of the series hail from many disciplines and walks of life. They include authors, musicians, athletes, political leaders, entertainers, entrepreneurs, and others who have made a mark on modern life and who, in many cases, will continue to do so for years to come.

These biographies are more than factual chronicles. Each book emphasizes the contributions, accomplishments, or deeds that have brought fame or notoriety to the individual and shows how that person has influenced modern life. Authors portray their subjects in a realistic, unsentimental light. For example, Bill Gates—cofounder of the software giant Microsoft—has been instrumental in making personal computers the most vital tool of the modern age. Few dispute his business savvy, his perseverance, or his technical expertise, yet critics say he is ruthless in his dealings with competitors and driven more by his desire to maintain Microsoft's dominance in the computer industry than by an interest in furthering technology.

In these books, young readers will encounter inspiring stories about real people who achieved success despite enormous obstacles. Oprah Winfrey—one of the most powerful, most watched, and wealthiest women in television history—spent the first six years of her life in the care of her grandparents while her unwed mother sought work and a better life elsewhere. Her adolescence was colored by pregnancy at age fourteen, rape, and sexual abuse.

Each author documents and supports his or her work with an array of primary and secondary source quotations taken from diaries, letters, speeches, and interviews. All quotes are footnoted to show readers exactly how and where biographers derive their information and provide guidance for further research. The quotations enliven the text by giving readers eyewitness views of the life and accomplishments of each person covered in the People in the News series.

In addition, each book in the series includes photographs, annotated bibliographies, timelines, and comprehensive indexes. For both the casual reader and the student researcher, the People in the News series offers insight into the lives of today's newsmakers—people who shape the way we live, work, and play in the modern age.

A Regular London Girl

At the 2012 Grammy Awards, all eyes were on twenty-three-year-old British singer Adele Adkins—known to the world simply as Adele—as she appeared onstage to sing her hit song "Rolling in the Deep." Just two months earlier, Adele had undergone vocal cord surgery, and many people wondered if she would ever sing again.

As Adele sang, it was clear that her voice was back, maybe even stronger than before. She belted out the popular love song with skill and passion. After an earthshaking performance, the audience gave her a standing ovation. That night Adele earned six Grammys, matching several Grammy Award records.

Adele's talent as a singer and songwriter has earned her more than awards, though. She has won the hearts of fans all over the world. As much as people love Adele's singing, they also like her sense of humor, thick Cockney (dialect spoken in parts of London) accent, and truthful personality. Though she is a pop star, she does not have the typical trappings of one. She does not wear skimpy, outrageous costumes or use high-tech special effects during her concerts. Adele just sings, and her phenomenal voice is as awe-inspiring as any flashy stage show. Though she is famous, she seems grounded and real. For all of these reasons, Adele is one of the most popular young singers of her generation.

A Star with Modest Roots

Before Adele became famous, she lived in a small apartment with her mother in one of the roughest areas of London. Though her family lacked money, they gave Adele plenty of support and encouraged her interest in music and singing. Meanwhile, the eclectic energy of London fueled Adele's creativity and gave her the opportunity to meet other aspiring and inspired musicians. Though her childhood was not perfect, she remembers her childhood years with fondness and gratitude.

Adele showed an extraordinary talent for singing at an early age. She liked to copy her favorite singers. Sometimes she performed for her family members or put on little concerts for her mother's friends. She loved being the center of attention.

Adele's mom did not have much money to spare, but she always found money for Adele's music lessons. Adele learned to play several instruments, including the guitar and piano. Though she did not live in a fancy house or have lots of material possessions, Adele did not feel poor. She had a loving family that encouraged her to do what made her happy—play music and sing.

Talent Opens Doors

Adele's talent earned her a spot in the BRIT School, a free performing arts high school in London. There Adele was surrounded by gifted students. She was able to play music and sing every day. She discovered she had a talent for songwriting, and she wrote what would become her first hit song ("Hometown Glory") when she was only sixteen years old.

After high school graduation, Adele posted the song, along with two others, on the social media website MySpace. Within the year, Adele was discovered by a record label executive who heard her music on the website. He offered her a recording contract. Adele, just out of high school, was now a professional recording artist. Her success and popularity increased at a sensational speed in the months to come.

Coping with Challenges

As her career blossomed, Adele faced personal challenges. Two of her romantic relationships ended in heartbreak. The breakups were painful. However, the intense emotion she felt inside fueled her songwriting and turned her sorrow into powerful, award-winning songs.

Besides disappointments in love, Adele faced other personal challenges. Her great love for singing and performing was

Adele performs at the 2012 Brit Awards. She had to learn to cope with stress and stage fright on her way to stardom and success.

accompanied by nearly crippling stage fright. As her fame grew, more was expected of her. She had to travel and promote her music. Because of her growing popularity, she had to perform in bigger and bigger venues. To top it off, most of her concerts were sold out. As her success snowballed, her stage fright only grew worse. When things got stressful, Adele sometimes drank too much wine and smoked cigarettes to help her cope. Over time Adele faced her fears and addictions. She learned to feel her stage fright and go onstage anyway. Once she began performing, her fear vanished.

A Regular Person Inside

Adele's perseverance and inner strength helped her overcome obstacles and push ahead with her career. Her natural talent also opened doors for her and earned her worldwide acclaim at a young age. By the time she was twenty-two years old, Adele had released two widely popular albums. Her many hit singles remained at the top of the record charts for months and months.

Despite being famous, Adele is very real person who, like most people, has faced her share of life's challenges. She speaks her mind, loves to joke around, and even likes to curse a bit. Adele is as charmingly down-to-earth as she is talented. Though she is a wealthy celebrity, she feels deeply connected to her roots. At heart she is still a working-class girl from South London, raised in a simple apartment by a single mother.

Chapter 1

A Gifted Child

Adele Laurie Blue Adkins was born in Tottenham, in North London, England, on May 5, 1988. Adele was a pretty, fair-skinned, strawberry-blonde baby with big green eyes. Her parents were Mark Evans and Penny Adkins.

Mark and Penny had met at a London pub in 1987. "She was a gorgeous-looking woman with real presence," remembered Mark, a tall, red-haired Welshman. "She was funny, too. She knew how to make you laugh, and she was intelligent and creative."[1] Soon after Penny became pregnant, the couple moved to a one-bedroom apartment two blocks from Penny's parents, Doreen and John.

When Adele was an infant, her dad played old records while rocking her to sleep at night. In 2011 Mark told a British newspaper that his taste in music—especially his love for jazz and blues artists such as Nina Simone and Louis Armstrong—had influenced Adele. "Night after night I'd play those records. I'm certain that is what shaped Adele's music."[2]

"It Was Kind of a Team Effort"

When Adele was three, her parents, who had never married, split up. Though Penny and Mark were no longer a couple and did not want to be in a relationship anymore, they remained on friendly terms. Adele's dad moved back to his hometown in Wales, where he found a place near his parents. He took odd jobs and eventually found work as a plumber.

Blue

When Adele was born, her parents were going to name her Blue. But at the last minute, Adele's mother decided to make Blue one of her middle names instead. Adele's parents had a special reason for wanting Blue to be a part of their daughter's name. They liked the blues, a type of music created by black Americans in the early part of the twentieth century. Blues music is known for its melancholic sound and sad lyrics. As baby Adele drifted off to sleep at night, her parents often played old blues records. Night after night, baby Adele listened to songs by singers such as Billie Holiday and Nina Simone.

Though she had dreams to go to art school, twenty-one-year-old Penny put them aside to raise Adele. For a while Penny worked as a professional massage therapist. She also worked as a furniture maker and an adult activities coordinator to make ends meet.

Though Penny was a single mom, she had plenty of help. Her parents often cared for Adele when Penny was at work. Adele adored her grandmother and called her "Nan." Penny had four siblings. Her two sisters, Kim and Anita, were a big help in raising Adele, too. "Mom's side is massive. All brilliant," said Adele. "Dominated by women and all really helping each other out, so even though she brought me up on her own, it was kind of a team effort."[3]

Child Musician

Adele was exposed to a wide range of music from an early age. Her mom loved music and wanted Adele to appreciate music, too. When Adele was only three, her mother took her to see the Cure, an English rock band. At home, Penny played her favorite

"Delly from the Block"

Adele's neighborhood of Tottenham, North London, is a multicultural neighborhood with a large African Caribbean population. The area is known for being one of the roughest areas in London. It has one of the highest rates of unemployment and poverty in the United Kingdom. The area is also known for a high rate of gang and gun violence. While she lived here, Adele was the only white student in her class. However, the color of people's skin did not matter to Adele. "I stopped noticing after a while,"[1] she said.

During her childhood Adele and her mom lived in other rough areas of London, including Brixton and West Norwood in South London. These experiences helped Adele develop a tough attitude to protect herself. "I always call myself 'Delly from the Block,'" said Adele. "You know J. Lo's 'Jenny from the Block'? [a song by Jennifer Lopez about feeling connected to her roots, growing up in a rough neighborhood]. I think I was just a thick-skinned girl from a very young age."[2]

Growing up in rough neighborhoods made Adele develop a tough attitude.

1. Quoted in Sylvia Patterson. "Mad About the Girl." *Guardian* (London), January 26, 2008. www.guardian.co.uk/music/2008/jan/27/popandrock.britawards2008.
2. Quoted in Jonathan Van Meter. "Adele: One and Only." *Vogue*, March 2012. www.vogue.com/magazine/article/adele-one-and-only/#1.

albums. In addition to rock music, Adele's mom also liked older folk and pop music by American artists such as Carole King and Roberta Flack.

Young Adele liked to listen to music on the radio and television. In 1992, when she was four years old, her favorite

R&B singer Gabrielle, known for her trademark eye patch, was a popular performer in Britain in the 1990s and one of Adele's idols when she was a young girl.

TV show was *Later… with Jools Holland*. The hour-long program featured five musical acts in a variety of musical genres. Her mother would let her stay up late every Friday night to watch the show, which aired from eleven o'clock to midnight. Adele watched and listened closely as the singers performed. Though it was far past her usual bedtime, she did not feel sleepy. She was particularly fascinated by their voices. "I used to listen to how the tones would change from angry to excited to joyful to upset."[4]

The same year, Adele's mom bought her a toy guitar. Adele strummed the strings on the small, red plastic guitar and imitated the singers she admired. She liked the singer Gabrielle, a popular rhythm-and-blues (R&B) singer known for wearing an eye patch (because she had an eye condition commonly called "lazy eye"). When Adele was five, her mom let her stand on the table at dinner parties and sing songs by the performer. "She just thought I was amazing,"[5] said Adele.

Adele had fun putting on a show for her mom's friends. When she finished a song, everyone clapped and told her what a good singer she was. She enjoyed the attention, and she especially liked how her singing seemed to make people happy.

"The Best of Both Worlds"

Adele enjoyed being a part of a big, extended family. Though she was an only child, she was not lonely. "I had, like, 30 cousins living down the road," recalled Adele, "so I'd go and see them, always arguing and hating to share, then I'd be back home to my tidy room and unbroken toys and no fighting over my Barbie. It was like I had the best of both worlds."[6]

Because of her large family, Adele learned to talk loudly and speak up for herself. "You had to fight to get your voice heard because everyone was screaming and chatting at the same time," recalled Adele. She was talkative in school, too. She had a good sense of humor and liked to kid around with her friends. "I was always the joker,"[7] she said.

Fond Memories

On summer break from school, Penny took Adele to visit her father in Wales. Wales is a country to the west of England, on the same island of Great Britain in the United Kingdom (UK). The

The Spice Girls, a popular British pop group in the 1990s, were an early influence on young Adele.

drive was not far. In a little over three hours, Penny could drive from London to Mark's home in Wales.

Adele developed a close bond with her paternal grandparents in Wales, John and Rose Evans. They had a big Victorian house in the seaside town of Penarth. For a while Mark and his father ran a café in a nearby amusement park. Adele liked visiting her dad. He bought her ice cream, and sometimes they stayed in a travel trailer. Adele loved to swim, and she liked to spend days at the nearby beach.

On one visit to the Welsh seaside, Mark's family had a big scare when five-year-old Adele went missing. "She'd been on a trampoline," remembered Mark. "I'd gone to get us chips [French fries], and when I got back, my mum was hysterical. She was saying: 'Adele's gone, she's gone.' We were terrified someone had grabbed her."[8]

Adele's family called the police to help, and they all searched the beach. Eventually, Mark found Adele. She was looking at a boat she and her family had sailed on the previous day. She was unaware that people were worried and looking for her.

On another summer trip to visit her dad, seven-year-old Adele was particularly enamored with the Spice Girls. The world-famous British group was composed of women nicknamed Baby, Posh, Scary, Sporty, and Ginger. Adele liked to sing along with their songs. Sometimes she imagined that she, too, was a Spice Girl. "Even though some people think they're uncool, I'll never be ashamed to say I love the Spice Girls because they made me who I am,"[9] said Adele.

When Adele's dad heard her sing a Spice Girl song, he was amazed. She had a beautiful, powerful voice. "My God, Adele's really got it," Mark thought to himself. "She's going to be a huge star one day."[10]

A Childhood of Changes

Beginning in 1996 Adele's family experienced many changes. That year Mark and his long-term girlfriend had a son. They named him Cameron. Adele, eight years old, now had a half brother. The next year Adele and her mother moved to Brighton, on the south coast of Great Britain.

Almost two years later, when Adele was ten years old, she and her mother moved again, to a small apartment in Brixton, in South London. Later Adele and her mom moved again, to the nearby area of West Norwood in South London. Penny rented a flat (British word for "apartment") above a store that sold discount merchandise, on West Norwood High Street. Although some kids have trouble adjusting to even one move during their childhood, Adele reportedly "loved moving." She said, "I don't think of my childhood like, 'Oh, I went to 10 different schools.' My mum always made it fun."[11] Soon after moving to West Norwood, Penny got married. Adele now had a stepdad.

Another life change soon came to Adele. When she was eleven years old, her paternal grandfather, John Evans, died of cancer.

He was only fifty-seven. His death was hard on Adele, but the loss was especially difficult for her dad. Mark tried to numb his sadness with alcohol. "I hit the bottle so hard that I am pretty much oblivious to anything that happened to me for three years," he said. "I was in the darkest place you can imagine,"[12] Mark said.

As Mark's life spun out of control, he lost touch with Adele. "I got wrapped up in myself," said Mark. "I wasn't there for her. The alcohol affected my relationship with Adele. I regret it, and I always will."[13]

Though she did not know it, her dad was embarrassed by his behavior and did not want her to see him at such a low point in his life. "And all the time I thought, 'How can I do this to Adele?'" her dad said. "I knew she'd be missing her grandad just as much as I was because they had such a close bond. She adored him. Yet all I could do was drink and I'm so, so ashamed of myself for that."[14]

Inspired by Music

Sometimes Adele missed her dad, but she had a lot of distractions in South London. Her big family, friends, and music were joys in her life. Some of Adele's friends introduced her to R&B, hip-hop, and soul music. She especially liked Mary J. Blige, Lauryn Hill, Aaliyah, P. Diddy, and Faith Evans. Her favorite R&B singer was Beyoncé, lead singer (at the time) for the group Destiny's Child. Adele liked to sing along with Beyoncé's songs. The upbeat music moved her, and the lyrics inspired her to be strong. "She's been a huge and constant part of my life as an artist since I was about ten or eleven," said Adele. "I love how all of her songs are about empowerment. ... Go get yours. Go get what you deserve."[15]

Sometimes Adele was so inspired by her favorite singers, she copied their style. For example, when eleven-year-old Adele wanted a sequined eye patch like the one Gabrielle wore, her mom bought her one. When she wore the eye patch to school, some kids laughed at her. The next day she decided to leave the eye patch at home.

Beyoncé was one of Adele's favorite artists as a child because of her inspiring and empowering songs.

Soon Adele tried out a different look. She applied thick, black eyeliner that made her bright green eyes look cat-like. "From the age of 12, I drew my eyeliner on like a cat," recalled Adele. Because of her dramatic eye makeup, her friends had a special nickname for her. They called her "Delly-cat."[16]

In addition to R&B, hip-hop, soul, and pop music, Adele liked indie music, too (lesser-known musicians represented by smaller, independent record labels). "I used to be obsessed like that, I was a real indie kid, but I'd secretly go home and listen to Celine Dion. She's got proper ballads!"[17] Adele declared.

Adele liked any music that inspired her, and she liked to impersonate her favorite singers. She had never had vocal lessons, but she understood instinctively how to sing. Not only was Adele a gifted singer, but she played the guitar, bass, and piano, too. Adele's mom encouraged her to follow all of her interests and drove her to music lessons several times a week. Penny had put her own plans aside to raise Adele, and she wanted her daughter to have more than she did in life. "She was so young when she had me, she probably would have gone to university and done art or something," said Adele, "so she was always telling me to explore, and not to stick with one thing, like other mums."[18]

Chance at a New School

While her music lessons interested her, Adele did not feel as inspired in school. She often grew bored and sometimes skipped class. "From twelve to thirteen I was a Grunger [in Britain, someone who likes Heavy Metal or Hard Rock]," said Adele. "Dog collars. Hoodies. We used to go to Camden [the raw, style-centric North London street market] all the time because we were, like, 'so dark.'"[19]

Adele's mom was worried. She thought that Adele was getting in with a rough crowd of kids that encouraged her to misbehave and skip school. Perhaps, she thought, a school with a different sort of focus—on music and performance—would be good for her.

Penny talked to Adele about changing schools. Adele liked the idea. She asked her mom if she could enroll at the Sylvia Young Theatre School, a prestigious, private, performing arts school in London. Adele had a special reason for wanting to attend the school. One of her favorite artists, Emma Bunton ("Baby Spice" of the Spice Girls), had attended Sylvia Young.

Adele's mom told her that she could not afford the high tuition at Sylvia Young. At first Adele was disappointed, but her mom had another idea. She suggested that Adele apply for a spot at a prestigious—but free—performing arts school called the BRIT School. Adele had heard good things about the BRIT School. She liked the idea of going to school with other creative kids. She could spend lots of time playing music and singing. Adele was not sure if the BRIT School would accept her as student, but she wanted to try.

Chapter 2

Discovered!

When Adele applied to the BRIT School, she felt excited. In addition to the normal classes offered in regular high schools, this special performing arts school would let her do what she loved most: sing and make music. Adele did not know it at the time, but the school was to help her in other ways, too. It would nurture and fine-tune her musical talent. Beyond that, it would lead her toward opportunities that were bigger than anything she could have imagined.

The BRIT School

The BRIT School for Performing Arts and Technology is located in London. The acronym *BRIT* stands for the British Record Industry Trust. The school is partly funded by the United Kingdom's record industry, as well as private and government funding. Students focus on one area of study, such as dance, music, or musical theater. Students also study standard curriculum, including math, English literature, and history. Former graduates of the BRIT School include singers Amy Winehouse and Kate Nash.

Adele was excited by the possibility of going to a school where she could focus on what she loved most—music. But first she had to apply and get in. She carefully filled out the lengthy application, for which she had to answer several essay questions. She had to explain why she was a good candidate for the music program. She was also asked to list what instruments she played and to describe her singing ability. The school's administrators wanted to make sure that all potential students had talent and were committed to the study of music.

BRITISH RECORD INDUSTRY TRUST

PERFORMING ARTS & TECHNOLOG
S C H O O L

Principal: Ms. C. A. Rumney B.A.

Main Entrance

Adele enrolled in the BRIT School in 2003 so that she could further develop her singing, songwriting, and performing skills.

Although Adele had never taken vocal lessons, she had been a singer since she was a young child. People had praised her singing voice for as long as she could remember. She had taken music lessons, and she could play several instruments. Adele had the credentials the school was looking for, and she was thrilled when she learned she had been accepted.

She started the program in 2003 and was blown away: The BRIT School was radically different from public school. Teachers encouraged the students to perform and express themselves creatively. "It was like *Fame*," said Adele. "There were kids doing pirouettes in the ... hallway and doing mime and having sing-offs in the foyer."[20]

Adele thrived at the school. She developed her ability to compose music, and she sang every day. The ability to sing came naturally to her, and she got plenty of practice at the school. Adele

Star-Making School

Like Adele, many former students of the BRIT School for Performing Arts and Technology went on to become successful professional musicians. For example, Adele's former classmate Leona Lewis became a multiplatinum recording artist and three-time Grammy nominee. Another classmate of Adele's became a prominent musician, the female singer-songwriter and R&B singer known as Jessie J.

Adele's next-door neighbor Shingai Shoniwa and Dan Smith (together with drummer Jamie Morrison) found success with their indie rock band, the Noisettes. Other BRIT School graduates formed bands as well. Members of the pop band the Feeling and the indie rock band the Kooks also attended the school. The members of the hip-hop duo Rizzle Kicks met when they were classmates at the BRIT School. Popular female singers-songwriters who attended the BRIT School include Amy Winehouse, Kate Nash, and Katie Melua.

learned that her voice was a contralto. Located between an alto and a tenor, contralto is the lowest type of voice for a female.

Adele liked it that her teachers had real-life experience with the subjects they taught. "I never got bored, so I was never getting in trouble,"[21] she said. The BRIT School teachers taught Adele and her schoolmates practical skills to succeed in the music business, too. For example, the students learned how to promote their music on the Internet and manage their finances.

Adele was grateful to attend the school. "I'd hate to think where I'd have ended up if I hadn't gone to The BRIT School," she said in 2011. "It's quite inspiring to be around 700 kids who want to be something—rather than 700 kids who just wanna get pregnant so they get their own flat. ... My first school was great but I'd have a kid by now if I hadn't left. And as much as I'd like to have a kid I'm not ready for one now."[22]

"My Heart Exploded in My Chest"

Though Adele liked her new school, she sometimes had trouble getting to school on time. Her frequent tardiness got her in trouble. "I'd turn up to school four hours late," she recalled. "I was sleeping. I wasn't doing anything. ... I just couldn't wake up."[23]

On one day in particular, Adele learned a big lesson about punctuality. Teachers had chosen twenty of the most promising students to perform at a musical festival. The event was in Devon, a county on the southwestern coast of England—a four-hour bus ride from the BRIT School. On the day of the event, Adele again woke up late for school. She realized she had overslept and missed the bus to the festival. "My heart exploded in my chest. It was pretty horrible," said Adele. "I almost did get kicked out of the school for that. But now I'm always on time, and if I'm late it's always someone else's fault."[24]

From that day on, Adele made herself get to school on time. But even though she liked her school, and she loved to sing and play music, she was not sure if she wanted to be a professional musician. She thought she might go to college after high school, and then look for a job. "My friends were telling me, 'You're really good,'" recalled Adele. "It never dawned on me that I could possibly do this for a living and not have to support myself working in an office from nine-to-five."[25]

"There were some people at school who really pushed hard," said Ben Thomas, Adele's former classmate and current guitarist. "You could tell they really wanted it [to succeed in the music business]. Adele never really had that. But she was a great performer and everyone would be completely silent and in awe when she performed."[26]

An Awakening

When Adele was fourteen years old, she went to see American singer Pink perform at the Brixton Academy, a popular music venue in London. Adele was profoundly moved by the concert. She considered it a defining moment in her life. "I had never heard ... someone sing like that live. ... I remember sort of feeling

The music of legendary jazz singer Ella Fitzgerald helped Adele to develop her vocal range and singing style and inspired her to instill her own songs with a timeless quality.

like I was in a wind tunnel, her voice just hitting me. It was incredible."[27]

The next year Adele was inspired by another type of music. She and her friends went shopping at HMV, a popular music and

Etta and Adele

A dele considers Etta James to be one of her greatest influences. James was born Jamesetta Hawkins on January 25, 1938. She had a difficult childhood and lived in several foster homes while growing up. Despite the difficulties, she had an early talent for singing. When she was five she sang in a church choir in South Los Angeles. The choir director saw Jamesetta's talent and potential and gave her singing lessons.

Etta James was one of Adele's greatest musical influences.

When she was fourteen Jamesetta reunited with her mother and moved to San Francisco. Still interested in singing, Jamesetta formed a girl group called the Creolettes. She was discovered by musician Johnny Otis who recommended that Jamesetta change her name. She reversed the parts of her first name to create her new stage name: Etta James.

During her long career, James sang music in many genres, including R&B, soul, jazz, blues, and rock and roll. Her hits include "At Last" and "A Sunday Kind of Love." Etta James received many awards in her lifetime, including six Grammys.

In June 2009 Adele was scheduled to perform with James at the Hollywood Bowl in Los Angeles. James was ill and had to cancel her performance at the last minute. James died on January 20, 2012. Adele later wrote in her blog: "What a lady Etta James was. She was the ultimate original. Her voice was breath taking and her songs are reflections we all recognize in some way or another. Its an honour every time I hear her voice. ... Thank you to Etta James."

Adele Adkins. "Etta James." Adele blog, January 23, 2012. www.adele.tv/home.

entertainment store in the United Kingdom. There Adele saw a two-for-one sale on jazz CDs. Adele chose CDs by jazz legends Ella Fitzgerald and Etta James. "I bought them because I loved their immaculate hairdos," said Adele. "And Etta James's eyes, the original Amy Winehouse eyes! I loved the vintage look of it."[28] When Adele got home she played the CDs and was deeply moved by the heartfelt and soulful music.

Adele later came to view her discovery of the two jazz singers as a turning point in her appreciation of music. She was impressed that she could enjoy music that people had made so many decades before her time. She, too, wanted to be a singer who was timeless and memorable.

Adele never had formal vocal training. She taught herself to sing by carefully listening to singers she liked. She learned how to stretch her voice across the scales by listening to Fitzgerald, from whom she also learned to inject deep emotion in her music. Another singer, Roberta Flack, was a big influence, and Adele learned from her how to control her powerful voice.

Adele had her own ideas about singing, too. She had a wide vocal range and could sing in several octaves. However, she wanted to sing in a way that felt natural to her. She did not want to show off her vocal range on every single song. "It's more impressive, somehow, if you don't try to impress," said Adele. "Be natural with it. Say it straight."[29]

Imagining a Life of Music

Right around the time she discovered Fitzgerald and James, another singer Adele liked released her first record. In October 2003 Amy Winehouse, a BRIT School alumna, released her first album, *Frank*. It would become Adele's favorite album. Adele liked Winehouse's strong R&B vocals. She thought she was a great songwriter, too. Inspired by Winehouse's success, Adele began to imagine a life for herself as a singer, songwriter, and performer.

Once Adele decided to become a professional musician, there was no stopping her. In school she continued to write songs and amaze her teachers and friends with her talents.

Adele's BRIT School classmates Dan Smith, left, and Shingai Shoniwa, center, went on to form a band called the Noisettes, which also featured Jamie Morrison, right.

After school, back home on West Norwood High Street, Adele practiced singing and playing music. She was happy when a classmate at the BRIT School, Shingai Shoniwa, moved next door to her. Like Adele, Shingai was a talented singer and musician. Shingai and another classmate, Dan Smith, had formed a band called the Noisettes (which later became a successful indie rock band).

Adele liked having a good friend nearby who loved music as much as she did. Shingai inspired Adele and fueled her interest in singing and songwriting. "We lived right next door to each other on top of [a store]," said Shingai. "Awesome days. She had a piano, I had a drum kit. We always used to jam."[30]

Songs Inspired by Life

When Adele was sixteen years old, her mom had a serious talk with her. She suggested that Adele attend a university in Liverpool after high school. She also wanted Adele to learn to be independent, something that would be hard to do if she stayed in London near her mother. "She told me if I stayed in London, ran out of money and couldn't pay the rent, she would always be around to help me," said Adele. "And that's not learning to live on my own or standing on my own two feet."[31]

Adele hated the idea of leaving her mom. "She's my best friend. I'm such a mommy's girl,"[32] she said. Adele was also attached to her friends, family, and hometown. She told her mom she did not want to go. After a big argument, Adele ran to her room in tears.

Overwhelmed with feelings, she picked up her guitar. In less than an hour, she wrote the music and lyrics of a new song. Adele called it "Hometown Glory." She sang it for her mom and told her that she would stay in London. Adele later described the song as "a mixture of all my best memories of living in London."[33] She

TV Favorite

A dele wrote the song "Hometown Glory" when she was only sixteen years old. The song has been used on the soundtrack of several American television shows, including *Grey's Anatomy*, *The Hills*, *Skins*, *90210*, and *One Tree Hill*. In the United Kingdom "Hometown Glory" was played on several TV programs, including the soap operas *Hollyoaks* and *Coronation Street*.

Several other Adele songs, including "Rumour Has It," "Turning Tables," and "Set Fire to the Rain," have been featured on television shows. Adele's hit song "Someone Like You" has been played on programs as diverse as the dance competition *Dancing with the Stars* and the TV comedy *Glee*.

explained, "It's about being able to walk past a bus stop, a clothing store, a restaurant, a bar or a coffee shop and have memories of them. In Liverpool, I had no memories whatsoever."[34]

Adele was soon inspired to write another song. On her seventeenth birthday, she and one of her longtime male friends shared that they had feelings for one another. But just two hours later, Adele caught him kissing one of her friends. "I was, 'We're not even going out yet and you've cheated on me already!'"[35] said Adele.

Hurt and disappointed, Adele went home and poured her feelings into a song. She called it "Daydreamer." She explained, "It's about everything I was hoping he'd be and we'd be, but he would never be and we would never be. So it's me daydreaming about him."[36]

MySpace Demo

The next year, as a final class project at her school, Adele created a three-song demo (sample of her music) that featured "Hometown Glory" and "Daydreamer." One of Adele's friends helped her post the demo on MySpace. The demo caught on fast, and Adele quickly gained MySpace fans. She was surprised and excited. People she did not even know liked her music!

Within a few weeks of posting her demo, Adele received e-mails from several record companies, including Island Records and XL Recordings. At first Adele did not respond to the e-mails. She was busy studying for her final exams and planning her eighteenth birthday party. In addition, she was not very familiar with recording studios and had never heard of the companies. "I thought it was some dirty Internet pervert," she says. "I saw there were e-mails from Island and XL, but I'd never heard of them so I didn't call them back."[37]

The representative from XL Recordings asked Adele if she was signed (had a recording contract). Adele e-mailed him back and said, "Leave me alone, I'm organizing my birthday party."[38] She then told the man that he could e-mail her again after she graduated from school in June.

At the age of seventeen Adele posted her first recordings to MySpace and soon caught the attention of several recording companies.

The Meeting of a Lifetime

Three days after graduating from the BRIT School in 2006, Adele received another e-mail from the man at XL Recordings. By this time, Adele had heard through friends that XL was an indie record label. Adele told her mom about the e-mail. She encouraged Adele to meet with the people at XL. But, just to be safe, she suggested that Adele take a friend with her to the meeting.

Adele called the number provided in the e-mail from XL. After a brief phone conversation, she agreed to meet with Nick Huggett, an executive with the company. When she got off the phone, she felt both excited and nervous. What kind of questions would Huggett ask her? Why exactly did he want to meet with her?

On the day before meeting with Huggett, Adele decided to do a little more research on him and XL Recordings. "I Googled the guy's name as I was leaving to meet with him and saw who he represented."[39] Her heart raced as she stared at what she saw. XL Recordings was a major indie record label! The London-based company, owned by Richard Russell, had signed some of her favorite musicians, including Radiohead, the White Stripes, M.I.A., Peaches, and many other top artists.

An hour or so later, Adele met with Huggett and other XL executives. The meeting went better than she ever could have imagined. "We met; they liked me and [wanted to sign] me," she said of the meeting. "I feel bad telling that story because it was really that easy."[40] Although the meeting was a breeze, it came about because Adele had worked hard for years—practicing and playing music, singing, and composing. Now her dreams were unfolding before her eyes.

Chapter 3

The Making of a Star

When Nick Huggett at XL Recordings discovered Adele's music on MySpace, he knew he had found a great musician. He also knew that Adele needed a business manager before she could officially sign with XL. That manager had to be smart, experienced, and capable of launching and managing her career. The manager would also need to handle the business end of dealings with XL Recordings and others.

Huggett called up Jonathan Dickins, an experienced manager he trusted. He told Dickins about Adele. He praised her voice, personality, and songwriting skills. Huggett suggested Dickins listen to her demo on MySpace.

Dickins's curiosity was piqued. He did not have a MySpace account, so he opened one to hear Adele's demo. When he heard her vocals on "Hometown Glory," he was blown away. Adele's voice and songwriting skills were brilliant. Without hesitation, Dickins called Huggett back to arrange a meeting with Adele.

Big Decisions

Adele met with Dickins in June 2006. "We had one meeting and just got on great," remembered Dickins. "Generally it just clicked."[41] Adele liked Dickins, too. She like that he listened to her ideas. Even though she was eighteen and just out of high school, he did not treat her like a kid. Adele was excited when Dickins told her that he managed one of her favorite musicians,

The New Amy?

When Adele first launched her career, many people compared her voice and music to Amy Winehouse. In some ways, the comparison was natural—both Adele and Winehouse were white, British, and wrote and sang R&B, soul, and jazz music. Although Adele did not agree with the comparison, she was flattered by it. She liked Winehouse's music but thought they were very different artists.

At the time, it was widely known that Winehouse had a serious drug and alcohol problem. (She died of alcohol poisoning in 2011.) Because Adele was so often compared to Winehouse, some reporters asked Adele if she used drugs. Although Adele has been upfront about drinking alcohol and smoking cigarettes, she has stated that she has never taken an illegal drug in her life.

Amy Winehouse was an artist that Adele was often compared to early in her career.

British singer Jamie T. She thought that if Dickins could manage Jamie T's career, she was sure he could manage hers. So she hired Dickins in June and was signed to XL by the end of September.

Adele soon made another big decision—to be known professionally by just her first name. "I hate my second name, Adkins. It's just so boring and British," said Adele. Although she liked her middle names, she thought all four names together sounded like "too much of a mouthful. And Laurie Blue Adkins sounds a bit folkie." So she decided simply to go by her first name, also because she did not identify with her last name. "If someone went, 'Adele Adkins,' I wouldn't turn around," she explained. "If they say, 'Adele,' I say, "Helllooooo?"[42]

Debut Performance

After Adele signed with XL Recordings, Dickins and Huggett began planning Adele's first record release. They thought that "Hometown Glory" was Adele's strongest work. They intended to release the song as a single (a song that is released by itself, independent of an entire album). But first, Adele needed to get out and perform in front of a live audience. People needed to hear her music.

Dickins scheduled Adele to perform as an opening act for another of his clients, an up-and-coming singer and songwriter named Jack

Adele's earliest music, including her debut performance after signing with XL Recordings, was made with just her voice and her acoustic guitar.

Peñate. The show was at the Troubadour, a well-known London coffee house founded in the 1950s. A club in the basement offered musicians an intimate, acoustic performance space.

When Adele found out that she was to perform at the Troubadour, she was excited. The venue had featured many musicians at the beginning of their careers, including Paul Simon, Jimi Hendrix, Joni Mitchell, and Bob Dylan. Though she was only the opening and not the starring act, Adele knew that performing at the Troubadour in any capacity was a gigantic opportunity.

On December 7, 2006, Adele showed up at the Troubadour, carrying her acoustic guitar. She felt very nervous. Her stomach ached, and she worried she might even throw up. Adele had performed plenty of times in front of her family, friends, and classmates and teachers at the BRIT School. However, she had never before performed in front of a live audience in a commercial venue. "I went on first and I was on my own, and the whole room was packed," remembered Adele. "It was hot. It was disgusting."[43]

Despite her stage fright, she felt right at ease once she began singing "Hometown Glory." The noisy crowd stopped chattering and turned to watch Adele perform. When she finished her performance, they applauded with enthusiasm. Some of the people had tears in their eyes. Adele was happy that she did not goof up and that the audience seemed genuinely to like her music. "Oh, my God, this is amazing, can't live without it,"[44] she thought. Performing live was freeing for her, and she felt energized.

TV Debut

After her performance at the Troubadour, Adele began touring small nightclubs and other venues as Peñate's opening act. Meanwhile, her record company circulated copies of "Daydreamer," one of the songs on her MySpace demo. In late 2006 BBC Radio 1 (a British radio station) started playing the single. Adele's music was starting to get noticed.

Just a few months later, in June 2007, Adele was booked to appear on her favorite childhood TV show, *Later … with Jools Holland*. She was terrified. The idea of performing in front of the

Adele performs in Brighton, England, in 2007, one of several appearances in public and on TV that she made that year to build an audience for her music.

show's studio audience made her nervous enough, but she would also be seen by viewers all over the United Kingdom. To top that off, stars Paul McCartney and Björk were also on the show. They would watch her perform, too.

For the performance, Adele sat on a stool and held her acoustic guitar. When she received her cue from the announcer, she began singing "Daydreamer." She looked nervous as she sang—her big eyes were open wide, revealing her stage fright. She also looked pretty, though. She had short bangs, peaches-and-cream skin, and strawberry-blonde hair pulled back in a casual, upswept hairstyle.

Adele felt less nervous as she continued with the song, and in the end she delivered a perfect performance. She also performed one of her newer compositions, "Cold Shoulder." After the show, Adele was excited to meet Björk and McCartney. Adele especially liked McCartney. He was warm and friendly and complimented her performance.

In December Adele appeared on another British TV talk and entertainment show, *Friday Night with Jonathan Ross*. Though Adele again got stage fright before the show, she pushed through her fear. She knew that once she started singing, she would be fine. She loved to sing, and she wanted people to hear her music.

Besides making TV appearances and performing in clubs around London, Adele had other work to do. The executives at XL Recordings wanted her to write songs—enough to make up an entire album. Adele felt worried. "I've always liked writing songs. But when I suddenly had to, I was dry and couldn't come up with anything," she said. "I was very nervous because I thought the label [record company] would say I wasn't ready."[45] Adele was not sure how or where she would find inspiration for new songs.

Heartbreak Leads to New Material

For several months, Adele had been dating a man from London. The man (whose identity has never been revealed) was a few years older than her. One day in 2007 a friend of Adele's told her that her boyfriend was cheating on her. Adele was furious and felt betrayed. She confronted her boyfriend in a nightclub. Adele explained:

We had a full-blown fight ... in front of all our friends. Now, I hate making people feel awkward, so I just left, but he didn't chase me. I was running down Oxford Street, which has these gigantic, wide sidewalks that go on for miles, and I just remember saying to myself, "Where are you going? What are you doing? You're just chasing pavements ... and you're never going to catch it."[46]

Adele did not want to lose the idea. She grabbed her cell phone out of her purse and sang the first line of a song into her phone's memo recorder. As soon as she got home, she ran to her room and wrote the song. She called it "Chasing Pavements."

The breakup sent Adele into an emotional, but creative, tailspin. For nearly a month, she stayed in her room. "I will sit in my room on my own for ages," said Adele about her breakups. "I can't be around anyone, I have to be on my own. And I'll write. That's how that atmosphere [in the songs] gets created."[47]

Adele did not want to talk to her boyfriend. She could not even face him in person to officially end their relationship. Instead, she sent him a text message. It read, "Babe, I can't do it no more."[48]

The Realities of Fame

After the release of *19*, people everywhere were talking about Adele. At first Adele got a kick out of her newfound fame. But the realities of fame soon started to soak in. When she went to the grocery store to pick up a few items, for example, fans followed her and took her picture. Near her home, professional photographers jumped out of bushes to snap her photo. Adele no longer had privacy. "I wanted to be a singer forever," said Adele. "But it's not really my cup of tea (fame), having the whole world know who you are."

Quoted in Anderson Cooper. "The Year of Adele." Video. *60 Minutes*, CBS News, February 12, 2012. www.cbsnews.com/video/watch/?id=7398480n&tag=contentBody;storyMediaBox.

"All The Words Came Out"

During a painful and intense three-week period, Adele composed nine songs. Her favorite one was called "Melt My Heart to Stone." She explained, "I just love singing it. When I wrote that song, I was crying. All the words came out in one take, as I was singing it."[49]

Combined with two of the songs from her MySpace demo, "Hometown Glory" and "Daydreamer," Adele had eleven songs. Her manager and XL Recordings were excited about her new songs. Her manager suggested she add one more song to the album, a cover of a Bob Dylan song called "Make You Feel My Love," which Adele loved and felt completed the album.

Now that Adele had an album's worth of songs, her manager and record company shifted into high gear. Executives at XL hired top people in the music industry, such as sound engineers, producers, and musicians, to put the finishing touches on Adele's work so they could release her first single.

On some songs, Adele worked with other composers to complete a song. For example, she would write and sing the vocals and then hum the music for an accompanying guitarist to copy. That person would then play with the arrangement and sometimes add to the composition. At first Adele was hesitant to involve others in her songwriting process. With experience, though, she learned that many songs grew stronger or more dynamic with input from other musicians.

Because Dickins's client, Jamie T, was very popular, they decided to release Adele's first single, "Hometown Glory," on Jamie T's own record label, Pacemaker Recordings. The record was released in the fall of 2007 as a 7-inch (17.78cm) Limited Edition vinyl record. On the B-side (flipside) of the record, listeners could hear "Best for Last," another heartbreaking song by Adele. Only five hundred copies of the single record were made. The initial record introduced Adele to listeners, music critics, and radio stations in the United Kingdom. Three months later Adele's second single, "Chasing Pavements," was released in the United Kingdom.

Adele channeled her personal pain into a three-week burst of creativity in which she wrote nine of the twelve songs on her debut album, 19.

First Album

On January 28, Adele's debut album, *19*, was released in the United Kingdom. Adele titled the album *19* because she was nineteen years old when she wrote its songs. In its first week *19* landed at the very top of the UK record charts. The *Guardian*, a major UK daily newspaper, gave Adele's album a five-star review. Calling her a "rare singer," the reviewer remarked on "the way she stretched the vowels, her wonderful soulful phrasing, the sheer unadulterated pleasure of her voice."[50]

When it was released in the United States (via Columbia Records), the album received similar praise. "Adele truly has potential to become among the most respected and inspiring international artists of her generation,"[51] said *Billboard*. *People* magazine also praised the album. "With a knockout voice that's

Adele debut album 19, which was released to critical praise in both the United Kingdom and the United States, topped the British music charts in its first week.

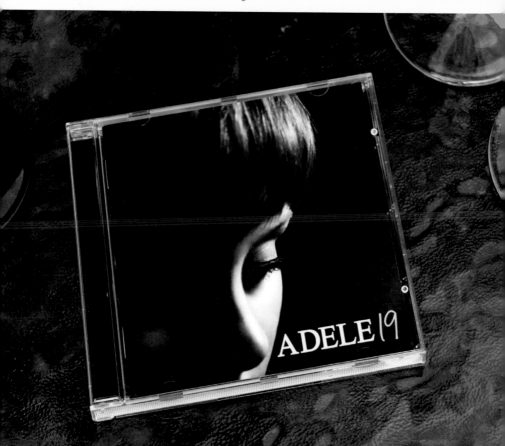

rich and supple, robust and sultry, it's hard to believe that this singer-songwriter is barely out of her teens."[52] When a reporter asked Adele's manager why he thought the singer was so well received so quickly, he replied, "She's just brilliant; I don't think there's any science to it. She is possibly the best singer, or one of the best singers, I've ever heard in my life." Added Dickins, "That voice is incredible."[53]

Chapter 4

More Heartbreak, More Hits

Adele's career was taking off: In the spring of 2008, she was preparing to launch her first world tour to promote her debut album. She was starting to become famous—people recognized her on the street and asked for her autograph. But despite her newfound fame and success, Adele felt a little lonely. She wished she would meet someone and yearned to be in love again.

New Love

Adele's wish to meet someone special soon came true. A friend of hers introduced her to a professional photographer in London. Even though he was seven years older than her, Adele was attracted to the man right away, and they began dating. When members of the media asked Adele if she was seeing anyone, she did not tell them about her new love. She was very private about her personal relationships. She also wanted to respect the privacy of her new boyfriend. However, the media was relentless in its pursuit to discover anything they could about Adele's love life.

Eventually, one publication revealed the man's identity. *Heat*, a British entertainment magazine, was the first to report that the relationship was with a professional photographer named Alex Sturrock. Many more credible new sources, such as the *New York Times Magazine* and the *Telegraph* (a UK newspaper), soon reported it also. When Adele met Sturrock, he was working for

Vice (an international magazine that covers arts and culture). He had also worked as a photographer for the *Guardian*.

Soon after meeting Adele, Sturrock took many professional, studio photographs of her. In many of the shots, Adele looked glamorous. They showed her with fully styled hair and makeup and wearing designer clothing. Besides showing the glammed-up, celebrity side of Adele, Sturrock managed to capture her personality, too. Many shots, posted on Sturrock's professional website, showed Adele laughing or hamming it up for the camera.

Given how close the two had become, Adele had mixed feelings as she prepared for her upcoming record tour. Her feelings for Sturrock had grown strong. "They spent all their time together—and when they weren't together they would ring [call] each other constantly,"[54] a friend of Sturrock's told *Heat*.

Adele did not like the idea of being separated from Sturrock as she traveled the world for a year. Then she got an idea. She knew that Sturrock was an excellent photographer, so she asked him to be her official tour photographer. Sturrock agreed to take the job. Adele felt happy and relieved that she and Sturrock could continue their relationship as she traveled from city to city and continent to continent.

World Tour

On April 23, 2008, Adele launched her world tour. *An Evening with Adele* began in Cardiff, Wales. Adele performed in cities around the world, including London, Paris, Berlin, and Amsterdam. While Adele was well known in Europe, she was lesser known in North America. Performances were scheduled for Toronto and Quebec, in Canada, and in many U.S. cities, including Seattle, Nashville, Detroit, and Washington, D.C. The concerts were intended to introduce North American audiences to Adele.

Sturrock accompanied Adele on most of her gigs and took pictures. Adele liked having him with her, as launching her tour was exciting but scary. "It starts from the minute I wake up," said Adele, referring to the stage fright she continued to feel, despite the fact that she was no longer new to performing. "I mean, I just

Adele performs in Amsterdam on the European leg of her first world tour in July 2008.

try and putter around and keep myself busy and stuff like that." She feared she was not "going to deliver … people aren't going to enjoy it … that I'll ruin their love for my songs by doing them live. I feel sick. I get a bit panicky." Adele got so nervous before a show that she sometimes vomited. "Projectile," she admitted. "Yeah … it just comes out."[55]

The more famous Adele became, the more nervous she was before a show. Once onstage, though, she relaxed and did not feel afraid at all. She discovered that chatting and joking with the audience helped calm her nerves. If she was nervous, she admitted it to the audience. She shared whatever she was thinking or feeling. Sometimes she talked about the song she was about to sing and shared details of the events that inspired the song.

Audience members liked Adele's chatty and amusing banter during a concert. They appreciated that she was honest and real with them. It made them feel closer to her, like she was a good friend, sharing what was on her mind. Besides being personable and funny, Adele always gave her audiences a great show. "I feel more at ease onstage then when I'm walking down the street," said Adele. "It's like singing in the shower at home. I love entertaining people."[56]

Adele put all of her energy into every performance. She knew her fans had paid their hard-earned money to see her show, and she did not want to let them down. Each time Adele sang one of her songs of heartbreak, she emotionally revisited the painful time in which she wrote the song. Touring was stressful, and performing night after night was challenging.

Coping with Stress

In the evening, after a performance, Adele liked to unwind with Sturrock. She enjoyed drinking wine and smoking cigarettes. Sometimes she drank too much to cope with the stress of touring. Sturrock kept Adele company and joined in the partying. According to *Heat*, the couple shared a hotel room during the tour. "He's a very normal guy and they'd laugh a lot together, eat junk food and ignore the fact that her career was about to go stratospheric,"[57] a friend of Sturrock's told *Heat*.

Because Sturrock spent so much time with Adele, he was able to take candid and sometimes intimate photos of her. He snapped photos of her onstage performing, but he also took more casual photos of her, too. He photographed her hanging out on her tour bus, joking around with red heart stickers stuck all over her face, sticking her tongue out at the camera, wearing a facial "mud mask" with curlers in her hair, and lounging in bed in her hotel room reading a comic book. Sturrock was good company to Adele and made the tour more fun.

U.S. Debut

After making several appearances around the United Kingdom, it was time for Adele to make her debut in the United States. There all of her shows had already sold out. On May 28 Adele performed at the Roxy Theater in Los Angeles. She was excited to come to the United States and was surprised that so many people had heard of her. "It's so weird to come all this way to do shows, and have them sell out," said Adele. "It's ridiculous and amazing how many people want to talk to me."[58] Adele still felt like an ordinary person from South London. Meanwhile, photographers, members of the media, and her fans were all treating her like the celebrity she had become.

As Adele traveled the United States, her record sales increased in other parts of the world. *19* received great reviews from music critics everywhere. As radio stations played Adele's hit singles, like "Hometown Glory," sales of *19* increased. Adele's career quickly picked up speed. "The reviews were incredible," said Adele's manager. "The reviews were so good in some of the markets it was like I'd written them myself."[59]

Mixed Feelings

Toward the end of the summer 2008, Sturrock decided to return to his life and work in London. Adele did not want to be separated from him, though. She felt torn between her career and the man she loved. In addition, she was homesick and tired from her intense tour schedule.

Adele made a drastic decision. Casting her career aside, she canceled the remainder of her U.S. tour and returned to England to be with Sturrock. "I was drinking far too much and that was kind of the basis of my relationship with this boy," Adele later revealed in an interview with *Nylon* magazine. "I couldn't bear to be without him, so I was like, 'Well, OK, I'll just cancel my stuff then,'" she said about her decision, which she regretted in hindsight. "I can't believe I did that," she said. "It seems so ungrateful."[60]

Adele's decision to cancel the rest of her tour shocked her road crew. The many people who worked with her—musicians, technical assistants, managers, and other support staff—had rearranged their lives to tour with her. Now they all had to return home. The future of the *19* tour was uncertain.

Adele's impulsive decision also upset her managers. She was a relatively new artist, especially in North America. Her action immediately created a lag in her record sales. Adele's career appeared to be in jeopardy.

A Lucky Break

Adele's relationship with Sturrock continued to have ups and downs. According to a source interviewed by *Heat*, though Adele and Sturrock shared her London flat, he still did not want to commit to her or call her his girlfriend. For several months Adele did some soul searching and came to regret her decision to quit touring. She worked with her manager to reschedule her U.S. engagements and continue with her record tour in 2009.

Meanwhile, in October 2008, Adele landed a great opportunity. She was asked to perform on *Saturday Night Live*. Each weekly episode of this long-running live TV show features comedy skits and a musical act. Fortunately for Adele, the timing was just right for her *Saturday Night Live* appearance. The U.S. presidential election was a month away, and Republican vice presidential nominee Sarah Palin was booked to appear on the show the very same night. Popular comedian Tina Fey also appeared on the program to spoof Palin. Audiences were excited to see Fey play Palin, who had been the

*Adele's appearance on an episode of **Saturday Night Live** in October 2008 boosted her popularity in the United States.*

butt of many jokes during the heated campaign. "Sarah Palin made my career by coming on that show,"[61] said Adele. Indeed, Palin's performance drew an estimated 17 million viewers.

The wide television exposure revived and boosted Adele's popularity in the United States. In the week after the *Saturday Night Live* episode aired, *19* soared to number eleven on the *Billboard 200* and soon won the number one spot on the U.S. music charts. As record sales flourished, Adele's international popularity skyrocketed.

Diamonds Are a Grammy Winner's Best Friend

Near the end of 2008, Adele received several major awards. She became the first recipient of the Brit Awards Critics Choice Award and was named the number one predicted breakthrough act of

2008. Adele also won the British Broadcasting Company (BBC) annual end-of-year "Sound Of" poll.

In December Adele's manager called her with more exciting news. She had been nominated for four Grammy Awards. Adele could not believe it. It was a great honor to be nominated for one Grammy, let alone four. Adele felt happy but overwhelmed. "I locked myself in the bathroom and cried for an hour!" she said. "Then my agent, who was crying, too, came over."[62] Adele and Dickins celebrated the monumental moment in Adele's career with a bottle of champagne.

In February 2009 twenty-year-old Adele prepared for the 2009 Grammy Awards. She usually liked to dress casually, but for the big event she received fashion guidance from *Vogue* magazine's editor in chief, Anna Wintour. "I'll go proper glam," Adele told Wintour. "Lots of diamonds!"[63] Adele requested that the dress be black, her favorite clothing color. She wore a black satin dress by designer Barbara Tfank and a diamond brooch by Stephen Russell. High heels hurt Adele's feet, but she was crazy about designer Manolo Blahnik's stiletto-heeled shoes, made popular by the chic TV character Carrie Bradshaw of *Sex and the City* (one of Adele's favorite TV shows). So, to top off her Grammy outfit, Adele wore Manolos embellished with diamonds.

That evening Adele was thrilled to win two Grammys, for Best New Artist and Best Female Pop Vocal Performance (for "Chasing Pavements"). Sturrock accompanied Adele to the Grammy Awards and snapped photos of her at the event.

When Adele won her first award, she went backstage and called her mother in England. (Adele had asked her mom not to attend the awards program. It made her nervous to have her mom around when she was working.) When she shared the good news, her mom screamed. "She's the most supportive mum ever. She's my best friend," said Adele a short time after the event. "Hopefully I'll sell 20 million records and she'll never have to work again."[64]

After the Grammy Awards show, Adele had some time off. She settled back into her apartment in London. There she and Sturrock continued to have relationship problems. "It just stopped being fun," said Adele. "We'd just bicker over a cup of tea or the fact that my lighter wasn't working. ... All my friends, everyone

A glamorous Adele shows her surprise at winning the awards for Best New Artist and Best Female Pop Vocal Performance at the 2009 Grammy Awards.

I worked with, no one liked him, because I acted different when I was around him."[65]

In June 2009 Adele returned to the United States to perform and complete her tour. Meanwhile, Sturrock stayed behind in

Something for Herself

Shortly after winning two Grammy Awards in 2009, Adele did something unusual for an award-winning celebrity. For a short time she worked in a small record store in London. There she sorted and labeled CDs in the back of the shop. Adele's coworkers could not understand why a wealthy, world-famous, Grammy-winning celebrity like Adele wanted to work in a record store. "They were baffled by it," said Adele. She took the job to stay grounded amidst her fame. She wanted to keep in touch with new music and remember life as a nonfamous person. In addition, Adele wanted to have a normal "first job" experience. Because she had launched her music career just out of high school, she had never had a first job like most young people. Adele did not tell anyone, especially members of the media, about her job. "No one knows I [worked at the record store], no one knows," said Adele. "I just did it for myself."

Quoted in Anderson Cooper. "The Year of Adele." Video. *60 Minutes*, CBS News, February 12, 2012. www.cbsnews.com/video/watch/?id=7398480n&tag=contentBody;storyMediaBox.

England. Adele had mixed feelings for Sturrock. She loved him, but he still refused to commit to her. Sometimes she was not sure what she felt for him. Though they did not officially break up, the relationship appeared to be over, and the couple parted ways.

Doing What She Does Best

Adele was disappointed about her breakup. Despite her pain over the failed relationship, she took comfort in the fact that, at twenty-one years old, her career was back on track. She was more famous than ever and had hit singles at the top of the record charts. Meanwhile, her album, *19*, went gold (five hundred thousand copies of the record had been sold).

Adele greets fans outside of the Ed Sullivan Theater in New York at her appearance on The Late Show with David Letterman, *one of many television appearances that helped her build a following in the United States.*

Adele's popularity in the United States climbed rapidly, especially after she made guest appearances on TV shows such as the *Late Show with David Letterman*. She also tried her hand at new experiences, such as appearing on the comedy-drama *Ugly Betty*. Although she learned a lot from the experience, she ultimately did not like acting. "I cannot watch it," said Adele of her appearance on *Ugly Betty*. "I play myself, but I was so sort of uncomfortable that I sound like an American putting on an English accent. I sound like Dick Van Dyke. I am the worst actress of all time. I'm like a ... cardboard box!" After *Ugly Betty*, Adele pledged to focus only on what she did best. "I am a singer. I will stick to what I am good at and not spread myself thin and become mediocre at everything I do."[66]

Heartbreaking News

Though her career was soaring, Adele was not completely happy. Sometimes she missed her ex-boyfriend, especially the close friendship and special connection they shared. It was lonelier touring without him. But in April she received upsetting news. A friend of hers told her that Sturrock was seeing someone new. Adele's heart sank. Her friend had more news to share. Not only was Sturrock seeing someone, he was engaged to be married! Adele was crushed. Part of her had hoped that her relationship with Sturrock could be rekindled. But when she heard that he was engaged, she gave up all hope.

Though she was heartbroken, Adele pushed on with her professional obligations. She did not want to let her fans down. She gave each audience her best possible performance as she completed her world tour. In July, after a final performance in Rotterdam, Netherlands, a brokenhearted Adele returned home.

Rough Landing

Back in London, the day-to-day reality of Sturrock's engagement hit her even harder. He was not there to hang out with anymore. He was no longer living with her, and she could not call him to

Rolling in the Deep
with Adele

Adele was devastated when her relationship with photographer Alex Sturrock came to an end. After the breakup she
turned to her other great love—music—to process her painful
and complex feelings. Through writing music and lyrics, Adele
expressed love, bitterness, pain, resentment, anger, and even
gratitude. The result was an emotional release for Adele that
resulted in the album *21*.

Adele expressed her hurt and angry feelings in one song in
particular, "Rolling in the Deep." In the UK, to "roll deep" is a
slang expression that originated in the rap or hip-hop culture.
To roll deep with someone means that you always have the
other person's back. A person with whom you roll deep will
always defend you and be there for you through thick and
thin. Before their breakup, Adele felt that she and Sturrock
rolled deep. "That's how I felt, you know, I thought that's what
I was always going to have, and um, it ended up not being the
case," said Adele. She put her own spin on the slang phrase
"roll deep" and called the song "Rolling in the Deep."

Other songs on *21* revealed more positive, tenderhearted
emotions. "Someone Like You," expressed sorrow, personal
reflection, but also goodwill toward her former boyfriend. The
breakup was difficult but meant to be. Adele was grateful to
Sturrock for the good changes he brought to her life—and
ultimately hoped he would find happiness.

Quoted in *Culture* (blog), *Rolling Stone*. "Adele on '21': 'The Songs on Here Are the Most
Articulate I've Ever Written." February 17, 2011. www.rollingstone.com/culture/blogs/
rolling-stone-video-blog-adele-on-21-the-songs-on-here-are-the-most-articulate-ive-ever-
written-20110217?page=2.

come over. Their relationship was really over, and he had really
moved on. Adele felt incredibly sad about losing him. She was
also furious at him. The last time she saw him, he had said things
that upset her. Adele reported he predicted that her "life was
going to be boring, and lonely and rubbish"[67] and that she was a

Adele attends the VH1 Divas performance in New York in September 2009, after a difficult breakup resulted in another period of intense songwriting.

weak person if she left the relationship. He also called her needy, which made her especially angry.

Though she was hurt, insulted, and angry, Adele did not call Sturrock or talk to him in person about her feelings. Instead, she went into seclusion in her home in South London. Like she had after her last breakup, she poured her feelings into songwriting. In a short, intense time, Adele composed several songs. One song in particular moved Adele deeply as she wrote it. She explained that she cried as she wrote "'Someone Like You' [which] was about him getting engaged really quickly after we broke up. And I wrote that to feel better about myself really, and it was about trying to convince myself that [I] will meet someone else, and I will be happy."[68]

A few weeks later Adele looked back on all the songs she had written. She knew she had some very good ones. However, she worried that she did not have the one big song that would complete the record. As Adele reflected on what her ex had told her when they were parting ways, she got angrier and angrier. "It takes a lot of [stuff] to get me upset and crazy, and so when I'm about to get angry, I can really feel my blood flowing around my body."[69] This is how Adele felt when the last song for the album came to her. She called it "Rolling in the Deep."

Turning Huge Pain into Huge Hits

When Adele shared her new songs with Nick Huggett at XL Recordings, he was impressed. From Adele's perspective, she had pushed through her pain and expressed her darkest and saddest feelings through music. The songwriting process had been healing for her. From Huggett's perspective, Adele had written extraordinary and powerful new music. He knew that her fans would love the new songs.

Huggett and XL executives met with Columbia Records and discussed the release of a second album. For the next several weeks, Adele collaborated with producers and composers to polish and complete the album. She particularly enjoyed working with producer and composer Paul Epworth. Adele collaborated with him on the production of "Rolling in the Deep." At first Adele did not want to work with Epworth. She had her own understanding of the song and her own unique musical style. However, after spending a few hours with him, she trusted him. "It ended up being a match made in heaven really,"[70] she said.

Adele thought that she grew as an artist while collaborating with Epworth. "He brought a lot out of me," she said. "He brought my voice out as well—there's notes that I hit in that song ["Rolling in the Deep"] that I never even knew I could hit."[71]

Near the end of 2010, the song was released as a single and was immediately praised by music critics as well as cultural historians. "From its opening raw guitar strum to its soaring, thunderous climax, Rolling in the Deep recapitulates the entire history of black music," said Camille Paglia, a professor of humanities and media studies at the University of the Arts in Philadelphia. "We hear the percussive accents of early rural Southern blues, with its hand-clapping and foot-stomping, along with a defiant touch of Native American war drums." Paglia also remarked that the song evoked other phases in African American music, such as gospel, jazz, and blues, and even "the 'call and response' format that has been traced from field songs under slavery all the way back to west African communal ritual."[72] Music reviewers felt the song's power, too. Edna Gundersen, a writer for *USA Today*, commented, "Pain, expressed in a powerhouse voice of mature emotional depth, never felt this good or proved this lucrative."[73]

Falling Tears

"Rolling in the Deep" was a major success. Adele had even more to offer her fans—another song about her breakup called "Someone Like You." (The completed version of the song was cowritten by Dan Wilson, who also played the piano on the song.) The song was wildly popular—in the UK "Someone Like You" became Adele's first number one single, and it stayed in the number one position for five weeks. When the single was released in the United States, it jumped to the top of *Billboard*'s Hot 100 chart (which measures record sales and radio play of an individual

Adele performs an emotional and moving rendition of "Someone Like You" at the MTV Video Music Awards in August 2011.

song) and stayed at the top for weeks. Adele now had two hit singles at the top of the music charts. "The songs are so powerful and accessible," said Ken Ehrlich, executive producer of the Grammy Awards. "You can be a 14-year-old girl or a 60-year-old guy and love those songs."[74]

"Someone Like You" was especially popular because of the emotional nerve it touched in listeners—some got goose bumps, and many were moved to tears. As *Guardian* reviewer Sylvia Patterson put it, "Adele's bewitching singing voice has the enigmatic quality which causes tears of involuntary emotion to splash down your face."[75] Another reviewer called the song a "10-hankie wretch-fest."[76]

Adele thinks the song has been so popular because millions of people have shared the painful experience of breaking up with someone they still love. "When I sing 'Someone Like You,' I know that every single person in the room will be able to relate to it. That's where that emotional connection comes from," she said. "I have sympathy for myself, I have sympathy for them, they have sympathy for me, and I know that we are all there knowing exactly how each other feels. It's like a big pact. You can just feel it. You can slice it."[77]

By November 2011 the song had such a reputation for making people cry that it was even spoofed by comedians on *Saturday Night Live*. The comedy sketch showed a lone female office worker in the mood to cry after a work disappointment. At her desk, she puts on "Someone Like You." She starts sobbing. Other office workers join her—all crying once they hear the song. The song even makes the janitor and window washer cry.

Boston Globe reporter Beth Teitell wanted to understand better why "Someone Like You" makes so many listeners break down in tears. She interviewed several fans, music professionals, and music professors and concluded that beyond its sad lyrics, "Someone Like You" evokes a powerful and shared human experience. "You can approach a random woman, inquire if the ballad chokes her up, and in almost every single case, she will confide her own heartbreak,"[78] observed Teitell.

Teitell also interviewed Stephan Pennington, an assistant professor of music at Tufts University, who reported that the musical structure of "Someone Like You" is designed to emotionally compliment the sad lyrics and draw an even more powerful response out of a listener. Part of what makes "Someone Like You" so heartbreaking, according to Pennington, is the contrast between Adele's insistence that she will recover emotionally and the music itself: "It circles around the same notes, never resolving," Pennington explained, "never finding peace."[79]

Jimmy Kachulis, a professor at Berklee College of Music in Boston, agreed and pointed out that the song's power comes from its use of old musical arrangements that have been featured in some of civilization's most famous and beloved songs. Kachulis attributed "the song's power in part to its layering of simple blues-folk melodies over a classical-style piano accompaniment, a combination often used in hymns such as 'Amazing Grace.'"[80]

"Just Little Old Me"

Even as people were crying all over "Someone Like You," Adele's first single from the album, *21*, "Rolling in the Deep," also jumped to the top of the record charts in both the UK and United States—and stayed there for weeks. The phenomenal success of both singles was record breaking. In the history of the *Billboard* Hot 100, Adele was the first female British singer to have two number one singles from the same album.

Adele was a little astonished that people liked her songs so much. "I find it quite difficult to think that there's, you know, about 20 million people listening to my album that I wrote very selfishly to get over a breakup," said Adele. "The fact that so many people are interested in that, and want to cry to it, or want to feel strong to it, or whatever … it's just little old me."[81]

Not only did the public enjoy Adele's music, some reviewers commented on Adele's unique and genuine musical style. "Adele is not rock-'n'-roll. She is not self-consciously retro. She does not shimmy or shake. Hers is a plant-the-feet-and-belt delivery that has all but disappeared from the pop landscape,"[82] wrote interviewer Jonathan Van Meter in *Vogue*. Adele admits that her style of music does not fall into any particular genre—she just writes songs that she feels. "I'm not trying to be pop. I'm not trying to be jazz. I'm not trying to be anything," she said. "I'm just writing love songs. And everyone loves a love song."[83]

Adele performs in Munich, Germany, in March 2011 on her second world tour.

The Toll Fame Takes

In addition to loving her songs on the radio and in their homes, Adele fans flocked to see her deliver emotional performances in person. Adele launched her second tour, *Adele Live*, in March 2011 and was scheduled to perform in cities all over Europe and North America. Each time she sang one of her heartbreaking songs, it took her back to the time the song was written. "Even though my emotions aren't with my ex at all anymore … every show is pretty emotional," said Adele. "It takes a toll."[84] Singing to sold-out venues night after night proved to be stressful for Adele—both emotionally and physically. In fact, the toll on her health would be more extreme than anything she could have imagined.

Chapter 5

Career Crisis

The emotional and physical stresses of touring finally took their toll on Adele's health, and in February 2011, onstage in the middle of live radio show in Paris, she had a shocking experience. She felt something rupture in her throat, affecting her ability to sing. It was "like someone pulled a curtain over my throat," said Adele. "It felt like something popped in my throat."[85] Adele was worried. She had never had voice problems before. She had experienced an occasional sore throat or cold, but this time it was different. Adele knew this was serious.

"The Eye of the Storm"

The next day Adele flew to London to see her doctor. She was diagnosed with acute laryngitis. The doctor advised her to rest her voice. Unfortunately, Adele was in the middle of a concert tour. "I ... should've stopped singing f   months really. And properly rested my voice," she said. "B.   kind of impossible to do when you're in the eye of the storm."[86]

Adele rested her vocal cords for a short time. Meanwhile, the release of *21* in North America in March created a sensation in the music world. Like *19*, the album was named after her age when she composed the songs on the album. And, like her first album, *21* received great reviews from the critics. People appreciated how Adele's love songs were deeply expressive. In her lyrics, she spoke of many emotions, including bitterness, sadness, and thankfulness. *New York Times* writers Jon Caramanica, Jon Pareles, and Nate Chinen called *21* "the rare break-up album as scornful of

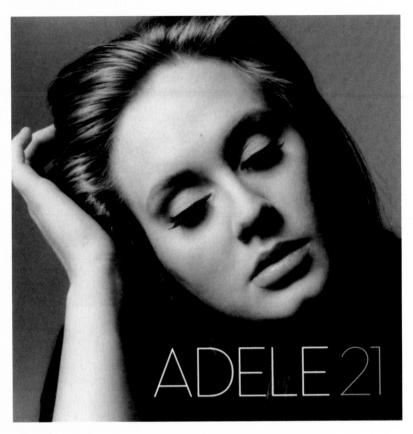

Adele's second album, 21, was released in North America in March 2011 to great critical acclaim.

the singer as her subject."[87] Another reviewer wrote that *21* was a "perfect album" that "floats beyond countries and time."[88]

As the buzz about *21* grew louder, Adele became anxious to get back on the road and perform. As soon as could sing again, she continued with her tour. Sometimes it hurt a little to sing, and she had a constant sore throat. Shortly before a concert in the United States in May, Adele again lost her voice. She felt frightened. What if she were to lose her voice forever? Adele's manager canceled several of her upcoming tour dates, and she took several weeks off to recover. To help herself heal, Adele stopped drinking. She cut back on her smoking. She cut out all of the foods that voice coaches and doctors warn singers to avoid, such as citrus fruit, dairy products, caffeine, fizzy drinks, and vinegar.

Adele did not want to let her fans down. She knew that many people had purchased tickets to her concerts, and she did not want to disappoint them. Adele rested her voice for a few weeks. Then she continued with her tour, not knowing that her health was about to take an even more serious turn.

Memorable Performance

Adele was troubled by the recent problems with her voice. Every time she performed, she wondered if her voice would hold up. Would she be able to hit the highest notes—or would she suddenly lose her voice completely?

On September 22, 2011, Adele took the stage at the Royal Albert Hall in London. Though she was a little nervous about her voice, she tried not to think about it. Adele felt excited. She had always dreamed of performing at the renowned concert hall, founded by Queen Victoria in 1871. And now, at the final UK stop in her record tour, her dream had come true.

Between each song, Adele stopped to talk to the audience. She told the story behind many of the songs on 21. She talked to the audience casually, just saying whatever popped into her head. Even though the circumstances behind many of Adele's love songs were sad, she managed to make the audience laugh anyway.

During the concert, a spotlight focused on a group of Adele's girlfriends in the audience. Adele pointed out her best friend, Laura, in the group. She told the audience that she had written the next song she was going to sing for Laura. The upbeat jazzy song, "My Same," played on the differences between Adele and Laura—and how their friendship works despite their differences. While Adele sang the song, viewers could see Laura in the audience, wiping away happy tears. In addition to the meaningful moment, Adele thought her performance at the Royal Albert Hall was one of the best performances of her career, and it helped ease her concerns about her voice.

Sudden Silence

Just a week after the Royal Albert Hall performance, Adele performed at her friend Laura's wedding. During one song, she opened her mouth to sing, but sound would not come out. Adele was scared.

After seeing a doctor, Adele was diagnosed with a polyp on her vocal cords. A polyp is an abnormal growth inside the body. Adele's polyp had hemorrhaged (ruptured and bled). It caused her to lose her voice. She was forced to cancel several concerts in order to let her vocal cords relax and heal. "I knew my voice was in trouble," said Adele, "and obviously I cried a lot. But crying is really bad for your vocal cords, too!"[89]

The word spread fast that Adele was having vocal cord problems. Many people feared she would never sing professionally again. Adele was concerned that her voice would change and get lower. Several prominent musicians, such as Elton John and Roger Daltry (lead singer in the rock band the Who), reached out to help Adele. They told her to go see world-renowned vocal cord specialist Steven Zeitels. The Boston-based doctor had developed a laser technique to stop vocal cord bleeding. Zeitels had performed the surgery on many singers, including Daltry, and Steven Tyler of Aerosmith. Adele flew to Boston to meet Zeitels, whom she fully trusted with her care.

After resting her voice and not singing for five weeks, Adele checked into Massachusetts General Hospital. On November 3, 2011, Adele underwent vocal cord surgery. Zeitels removed a benign (not cancerous) polyp from Adele's vocal cord. After the surgery, Adele went into seclusion in her home. Her doctor ordered her not to speak for two months.

Adele took Zeitel's words very seriously. She cared too much about her voice to take any chances. To keep silent, Adele found special ways to keep in touch with the people in her life. At home she used a notepad to communicate with her family and friends. Adele got a special app (application) for her phone that allowed her to type in her words, and the phone spoke the words to her friends. "Most of 'em you can't swear on, but I found this one app where you can swear," said Adele. "So I'm still really getting my point across."[90]

Adele's miniature dachshund, Louis Armstrong, stayed by her side as she healed. Adele came to enjoy spending time alone. For the first time since she became famous, she had time to think about her life. She also had time to process her feelings about past relationships. "It was like I was floating in the sea for three weeks," said Adele. "It was brilliant. It was my body telling me to fix me."[91]

An Instant Spark

During this time, Adele started seeing someone new: a man named Simon Konecki. Konecki, who was thirty-seven, was fourteen years older than Adele. He had a five-year-old daughter from a previous marriage. Once an investment banker, Konecki now ran a charity called Drop4Drop, which helps improve people's

Adele and Simon Konecki, right, attend the Grammy Awards in February 2012.

access to clean drinking water, something 1.2 billion people lack around the world. Konecki had attended Eton College, a prestigious boarding school in England for boys age thirteen to eighteen. He was big, strong, and gentle-natured. He had a full beard, a deep voice, and a friendly smile.

Konecki helped Adele recover from her vocal cord surgery, and both friends and family thought they were a great match. Like Adele, Konecki was down-to-earth and a bit of a homebody. Though he was wealthy, he preferred to hang out with friends and have a good meal than be with businesspeople or celebrities. He was a spiritual person and, like Adele, held liberal political views.

Adele liked Konecki's rugged, teddy-bear good looks. He resembled one of her favorite actor-crushes, Zach Galifianakis (who appeared in *The Hangover* and other movies). Adele also liked it that her celebrity status meant very little to Konecki. He was proud of Adele's achievements and thought she was very

Looking for Love

Most people do not know that Adele has tried online dating (meeting potential partners through a website or matchmaking program). In early 2011 Adele admitted to *Entertainment Weekly* that she had recently signed up with the popular online dating service eHarmony. Though she posted a profile (a description of her likes and dislikes, hobbies, and so on), Adele did not post a picture of herself, because she did not want anyone to date her just because she was famous and wealthy.

Many members in the dating community will only pursue another participant if they can first see a photograph of him or her. Because Adele did not post a picture of herself, she did not get any replies. Though online dating did not work out for Adele, she soon found love anyway. Just a few months later, Adele met Simon Konecki.

talented, but he loved her for who she was inside, not for what she did for a living.

Although Konecki was divorced when he and Adele started dating, rumors began to circulate in the media that he was still married. The *Huffington Post* and many other sources hinted at a scandal by reporting that Adele was dating a married father. Adele was quick to respond to the false reports on her blog, where she denied that her relationship with Konecki was at all inappropriate, and confirmed that he had been divorced for years. She also reported that she and Konecki had fallen head over heels in love.

Rebuilding Her Voice

Despite Adele's elation over finding new love, she continued to be nervous about her still-fragile voice. Compounding her nerves was the fact that in November, just weeks after her vocal cord surgery operation, she learned she had been nominated for six Grammy Awards. She was even nominated for the most prestigious Grammy, Album of the Year. When Adele found out about her nominations, she burst into tears.

The media also announced that Adele would perform at the Grammy Awards ceremony in February—less than two months after her surgery. Adele still was not supposed to speak, so she issued a written statement to the news media. In the statement, she said she was honored to perform at the Grammys. She also said she was excited and nervous.

Many people wondered if Adele was performing too soon after her surgery. Neil Portnow, president of the National Academy of Recording Arts and Sciences (producers of the Grammy Awards), spoke with Adele's doctor shortly before the Grammys. "All of us in the industry were concerned," said Portnow, who was comforted only by the fact that he had spoken with Adele's doctor, who assured him his patient would be up for the event. "[Zeitels] performs incredible medical miracle work ... and he told me that she was remarkably resilient and had done really well and that she would shine and soar."[92]

As the days leading up to the February Grammy Awards show approached, Adele slowly prepared herself for the performance. In late November Zeitels told Adele that it was time for her to begin building her vocal cords up again. Though she was not allowed to sing yet or talk, he told her to hum. He wanted her to start off very slowly and build her voice gradually. Adele began humming her favorite songs around the house. Eventually, she was allowed to speak, too, but only in moderation. She was instructed to rest her voice for several hours a day. In mid-December, Zeitels gave Adele permission to start singing again.

Adele had worried that her singing voice would not sound like her anymore. However, she was delighted when she heard it again. Her voice sounded great! However, it sounded a bit higher to her. Before the surgery, she had been singing with a polyp on her vocal cords. The polyp had made her voice sound a little lower and huskier. Now, it was easy to sing. "I used to always wonder will I hit that note, even when I wasn't ill," said Adele. "It's basically a clean slate in my throat. And it's just clear."[93]

A "Life-Changing Year"

Adele's many fans and friends in the music industry anxiously awaited her performance at the *54th Annual Grammy Awards*. Actress Gwyneth Paltrow seemed to speak for people both in the crowd and watching at home when she announced Adele that evening, saying, "We are so thrilled that once singular voice of hers is back and that she is ready to share it with us once more, right here, at the Grammy Awards."[94]

The audience was still and silent, awaiting the sound of Adele's voice. Had she healed from her vocal cord surgery? Would she be able to sing as well as before? Standing in a single, brilliant spotlight in an elegant, black Giorgio Armani dress, Adele began singing her hit song, "Rolling in the Deep." Her voice was as strong, or maybe even stronger, than before her surgery. Her performance was, as usual, without special effects, dance moves, or stunts.

Instead, she stood in one spot on the stage, gently rocking back and forth, lifting her arms in fluid, expressive hand motions as

Adele demonstrated her successful recovery from vocal chord surgery with a strong performance of "Rolling in the Deep" at the 2012 Grammy Awards.

she sang. Accompanied by her band and four backup singers, Adele hit every note. She stunned viewers around the world with her powerful, five-octave voice that can so skillfully convey the emotions of heartbreak. The audience was deeply moved by the

Bold Blunder

Shortly after winning six Grammy Awards in February 2012, Adele flew back to London for the Brit Awards. There Adele was honored with two more prestigious awards, for Best British Female and Mastercard British Album of the Year. Thunderous applause broke through the audience when Adele won the show's top prize, Album of the Year. "I'm so proud to be British ... and I'm so proud to be in the room with all of you," began Adele.

Unfortunately, the live broadcast was running long and the show's host, actor James Corden, was told to cut Adele's speech short. *Adele accepts the Album of the Year award at the 2012 Brits.* Adele was upset. She had wanted to thank a whole list of people in her acceptance speech. Adele was angry and not afraid to show it. She wanted to give the show's producers a piece of her mind. "You're gonna cut me off. Can I just say then, goodbye, and I'll see you next time around, yeah?"[1] Adele then made a bold, off-color gesture with her middle finger.

After the show, Adele told reporters that her gesture was directed toward "the suits" (executives) at the Brit Awards, not to her fans. "I was about to thank the British public for their support and they cut me off. So I'm sorry if I offended anyone, but the suits offended me."[2]

1. Quoted in *2012 Brit Awards*. ITV, February 21, 2012.
2. Quoted in Alanah Eriksen. "Brits Double Winner Adele Makes a Very Rude Gesture after Show Host James Corden Interrupts Her Final Winner's Speech." *Dailymail.co.uk*, February 23, 2012. www.dailymail.co.uk/tvshowbiz/article-2104544/BRIT-Awards-2012-Adele-flips-bird-James-Corden-interrupts-speech.html#ixzz1xEFnj42C.

performance. When she finished the song, the audience—many of them top stars in the music industry—gave her a standing ovation. It was one of the loudest and longest standing ovations in the history of the Grammy Awards.

Adele appeared onstage six more times that night—each time to receive a Grammy. During her many acceptance speeches, she thanked her mother, and also her doctor, whom she credited for saving her voice. By the time she won her sixth, and most prestigious, award, for Album of the Year, Adele was in tears. Always humble and real, a tearful Adele joked about wiping her runny nose, saying a sincere thanks and giving a thumbs-up gesture. As she accepted the trophy, she was filled with emotion. "This record is inspired by something that is really normal and everyone's been through it, just a rubbish relationship," said Adele with her thick accent and jolly sense of humor. The audience laughed and so did Adele. Her voice began to quiver as she held back tears and concluded her speech. "It's been the most life-changing year."[95]

"You Know You've Made It"

With her 2012 Grammy triumph, Adele became the sixth recording artist to win six awards in one ceremony. (The Dixie Chicks were the last to be awarded with six Grammys in one evening, in 2007.) Adele tied Eric Clapton for most awards won by a British artist in one ceremony. In addition, Adele tied her idol, Beyoncé, for most Grammy awards won in one year by a female recording artist.

Including her two 2009 Grammy wins, Adele was now an eight-time Grammy Award winner. On the live TV broadcast, viewers could see a close-up of former Beatle Paul McCartney. He stood and cheered, his arm raised in a wave to Adele. In turn, viewers could see Adele blowing a kiss back to McCartney. Seven News reporter Sally Biddulph of Australia pointed out the significance of this moment. "Her Grammy haul [is] now greater than the Beatles—and when one of them gives you a standing ovation, you know you've made it."[96]

Adele beams as she poses with the six awards presented to her at the 2012 Grammys.

The day after Adele's huge win, sales of her records skyrocketed. Her top hits were played repeatedly on pop radio stations. Sales of *21* spiked 207 percent. Sales for her first album, *19*, which had already gone platinum (that is, sold 1 million copies), also topped the record charts. Newspapers, TV shows, websites, and blogs around the world covered the story of Adele's record-breaking Grammy win. In the United Kingdom, Adele's homeland, the news of her win was especially welcome.

After enduring serious physical and emotional challenges, Adele had made an awe-inspiring comeback. Her powerful voice was back, and her fame reached new heights. Now Adele looked forward to taking some much-deserved time off and enjoying regular, noncelebrity life once again.

Chapter 6

Getting Real
with Adele

In a short time Adele has come a long, long way. She has sur-
vived serious life challenges and is now a wealthy, well-known
singer. Besides being a famous musician, Adele is a down-to-
earth, regular person. The real Adele wants the same things that
most people want—to be happy and healthy, have fun, do work
she likes, and love and be loved.

Sad Songs, Happy Girl

Many of Adele's songs are sad and serious. But in real life Adele
is quite the opposite. Adele is often bubbly and carefree. She
loves to talk, joke, and laugh. "She just comes across as very
approachable, just a normal English girl," says her assistant,
Rose Moon, "and so people say hello and want to talk to her
everywhere she goes."[97]

In addition to being outgoing, Adele has a great sense of
humor. She is known for having several distinct types of laughs.
Reporter Jonathan Van Meter spent several days with Adele,
interviewing her and getting to know her. "Within a span of five
minutes, I am introduced to several of the explosive laughs in
the Adele repertoire," he observed. "There is the high-pitched
hee! hee! hee! hee! hee!; the machine gun–fired *ha! ha! ha! ha!
ha!*; the single, startling *honk!*; and the full-throated, rip-roaring
cackle (it defies the alphabet) that she lets loose dozens of times
a day."[98]

Adele's happy, carefree demeanor is in contrast to the sad and serious mood of many of her songs.

Adele also likes to swear—a sharp contrast to her poised and elegant onstage demeanor. She "has one of the great dirty mouths of her generation," said Van Meter. "Get her going on a subject that raises her ire, and the obscenities fly like sparks off a welder."[99]

Quiet Times

Adele has a quiet side, too. When she is not working, she likes to hang out with her dog, Louis Armstrong, as well as partner Simon Konecki, friends, and family. She would rather relax in the comfort of her own home than go to a red carpet event. She would rather play Monopoly with her friends than make small talk with famous people at an exclusive music industry party.

Adele also enjoys spending time alone. In her spare time she enjoys doing many of the same things she liked to do before she became famous. Adele is a good cook, and she likes to bake, too. Her favorite thing to bake is cupcakes. To relax, she likes long, hot baths. Although she admits she sometimes enjoys "trashy reality TV," Adele especially likes movies. She watches several films every week. "I'm a very big movie buff," she says. "I know more about movies than I do about music—and I know a lot about music."[100] Adele likes all kinds of movies, from lighthearted romance movies to thrillers about gangsters and criminals. She is especially enamored of actors Al Pacino, Alec Baldwin, and Colin Firth.

Comfort and Style

Adele's is known for speaking her mind. She is also known for being down-to-earth and casual. She typically wears comfortable clothing when she is out in public. One of her favorite outfits is black leggings, ballet slippers, and an oversized shirt or sweater.

Though she usually likes to dress casually and comfortably, Adele has a glamorous and stylish side, too. Besides Manolo Blahnik shoes, Adele loves handbags, especially expensive bags by designers such as Chanel and Burberry. Now that she is famous, many designers simply give Adele expensive handbags and clothing. (Many well-known accessory and clothing designers do this; photos of stars carrying or wearing their items is great publicity for them.) Though Adele does not mind the freebies, she wishes the designers had been as generous back when she could not afford such expensive items.

When Adele does go shopping to purchase her own clothes, she insists on comfort. She usually chooses shops that sell comfortable clothing that is well made, stylish (but not trendy),

Adele sports her trademark casual style, including ballet flats, black leggings, and an oversized top, outside of a studio in London in January 2011.

and created from natural fibers. By matching comfort with style, Adele combines the best of both worlds.

"A Little Too Fat"

Adele knows herself well, and she is comfortable with who she is and what she looks like. However, women are often held up to challenging ideals of beauty, especially in the entertainment

Allergic to Vacations

A dele's strong sense of who she is and what she likes and does not like—with no apologies—is an inspiration to her many fans. For example, a reporter for *Marie Claire* magazine once asked Adele what the highlight of her best vacation was. Adele did not show off an interesting experience or exotic travel destination. She did not try to come up with a polite response just for the sake of the interview. In response to the reporter's question, Adele said exactly what she was thinking. "I don't take them (vacations)," she replied bluntly but honestly. "I'm allergic to the sun and get bored."

Quoted in Thelma Adams. "February Survival Guide." *Marie Claire*, February 2011, p. 113.

business. They are expected to be thin, stay in shape, and look like airbrushed models in magazines.

As a result, many reporters have focused on Adele's size. Because Adele is a tall (five feet nine inches), full-figured woman, some people think she defies the typical pop star mold. They wonder if she has had trouble being accepted in the music industry, when so many other pop stars are super-skinny.

Sometimes, her weight has been the focus of controversy, even cruel comments. For example, in February 2012 fashion designer Karl Lagerfeld made a controversial remark about Adele to the media. "The thing at the moment is Adele," said Lagerfeld. "She is a little too fat, but she has a beautiful face and a divine voice."[101]

Lagerfeld's comment offended many people. Some remarked that Lagerfeld would not have criticized a male singer about his body. They complained that because Adele is a woman, she is measured by different standards than a man.

Adele was annoyed by Lagerfeld's comments, as well as questions from reporters about her weight or body size. She simply says she has no interest in being skinny or having a "perfect" body.

While she would prefer the focus to be on her songwriting and performances, Adele has endured criticism and commentary about her weight.

"People who don't seem to have imperfections are boring," said Adele. "Everyone is meant to have imperfections. You're not human if you don't."[102] Adele holds herself to a different set of standards, most of which include the quality of her songwriting and singing. "I've never seen magazine covers and seen music videos and been like, 'I need to look like that if I want to be a success,'" she said. "I don't want to be some skinny mini. … I really don't want to do it. And I don't want people confusing what it is that I'm about."[103]

Indeed, Adele enjoys food, and, unlike other celebrities, refuses to be on a full-time diet or strict work-out regimen. Adele's complete acceptance of herself is an inspiration to her many fans, especially girls and women. She is a rare young celebrity who demonstrates that a woman can be happy with herself just as she is.

Family Relationships

In addition to loving herself, Adele also loves her family. She is happy she is finally able to give back to the people who helped her as she grew up—especially her mother. "Mum loves me being famous! She is so excited and proud," says Adele, "She had me so young and couldn't support me [there wasn't a lot of money to go round], so I am living her dream, it's sweeter for both of us,"[104] said Adele.

Adele loves to shower her mom with presents and gives her money to travel the world. Penny Adkins is adventurous and loves traveling. She can now do the things she did not have the time or money to do when she was raising Adele.

While Adele remains very close to her mother, her relationship with her father is strained. Mark Evans lives in Bridgend, South Wales, with his wife and son (Adele's half brother), Cameron. Mark made Adele very angry when he gave an interview to the *Sun*, a British tabloid newspaper, in 2012, reportedly without her permission. In the interview, her dad discussed Adele's childhood. He also told the reporter how much he loved Adele.

Adele was angry. She thought that her dad may have even been bribed by the newspaper to give them an interview. "I was actually ready to start trying to have a relationship with him," said Adele. "He's [expletive] blown it. He will never hear from me again."[105] One of the things that upset Adele so much was that her dad professed

Mark Evans, Adele's father, angered his daughter by revealing details of her early life in an interview in 2012.

to love her in the article, yet he has played a very minor role in her life. She was especially angry that her dad expressed his love to her in a publication, instead of telling her in person. "'I love her so much'? Really? Why are you telling me that through a newspaper?" Adele told *Vogue*. "If I ever see him I will spit in his face."[106]

Adele's father was upset by his daughter's reaction. "I can't believe she said that," he said. "It's devastating." He did not understand that Adele was angry because he communicated his private feelings for her through a reporter. Adele's dad has expressed deep regret about not being a better parent to his daughter. "What's done is done," he says. "I can't turn the clock back. I know I was a rotten father, but, in the end, she's made it. She deserves all the happiness and success in the world."[107] Adele's relationship with her dad is rocky, but she still keeps in touch with her paternal grandmother, Rose, and her half brother, Cameron.

Happy Times

Since the success of *21*, Adele has enjoyed taking some time off. She was in no hurry to compose or release a new album. Adele has said she wants her next record to be filled with happy, positive songs. Her first albums were inspired by heartache, but she wants future releases to be different. When asked if she will be able to compose songs without having her heart broken, she replied, "Well I hope so. 'Cause I'm madly in love and I don't want to be like 'Babe, I'm sorry, we've got to break up. I've got a new album to deliver.'"[108]

Adele hoped she would not have to break up with anyone anytime soon: In February 2012 she rented a ten-bedroom mansion on 25 acres (10ha) in Sussex, in South East England. Sussex is about a thirty-minute drive from Konecki's home in Brighton, and Adele took the property in part to be closer to him. Adele's house boasted a tennis court, helicopter landing pad, and two swimming pools. Staff members had their own separate cottage to live.

Adele's rental house used to be a convent. Sometimes Adele felt a little scared to be in the big mansion by herself. There were rumors that the house was haunted. The enormous old building with its many rooms and passageways made Adele's imagination run wild. When Konecki could not stay over, Adele asked her friends to stay with her, because she was uncomfortable being alone in the place. Adele employed two security guards to guard the mansion day and night.

Adele saw the rented mansion as a temporary residence, a place to live in while she and Konecki worked on renovating a new house,

60 Minutes correspondent Anderson Cooper, left, interviews Adele on the grounds of the mansion she rented in February 2012.

a seaside home in Brighton. They had solar panels installed on the roof to conserve energy. The eco-friendly home has sweeping ocean views and plenty of room and privacy. Adele and Konecki planned to make the house their first home together and thought the beautiful oceanfront property would be a wonderful place to raise children.

A New Chapter

It turned out that Adele would not have to wait that long to embark on that new chapter: In June 2012 she announced she was six months pregnant. "[I'm] delighted to announce that Simon and I are expecting our first child together," she posted on her blog in a message to her fans. "I wanted you to hear the news direct from me, obviously we're over the moon and very excited but please respect our privacy at this precious time."[109]

Though Adele had grown up as an only child, she had always been surrounded by lots of young cousins and other family members. She enjoyed the noise and fun chaos of a large family. She had always wanted a big family of her own. Adele felt close to Konecki's young daughter from his first marriage, and she could

Celebs Who Love Adele

Many celebrities are Adele fans. For instance, Beyoncé, one of Adele's favorite musicians of all time, reciprocates Adele's adoration and is a huge fan of her music. Madonna is a big fan of Adele's, too. She thinks Adele is brilliant and has expressed interest in collaborating with her on a song.

In 2012 *Twilight* star Kristin Stewart announced that Adele's albums *19* and *21* had given her special inspiration for her role as Snow White in the movie *Snow White and the Huntsman*. To prepare for the role, Stewart listened to Adele's music on her iPod. In particular, the deep feelings in Adele's music inspired Stewart. "The extremes of her emotion—like when she's got levity and she's got light, she's so light," Stewart told the *Sun*. "But when she's down it's devastating, and it just reminded me of the movie. I just love her."

Quoted in Gordon Smart. "Someone Likes You, Adele." *Sun* (London), June 1, 2012. www.thesun.co.uk/sol/homepage/showbiz/bizarre/4349984/Kristen-Stewart-reveals-she-listened-to-Adele-to-get-into-character-for-Snow-White-And-The-Huntsman.html.

see that he was a loving and responsible father. Adele thought he would be a great dad to any kids they had together, too. She gave birth to their son in October 2012.

Looking Forward to Love and Happiness

Adele has persevered through hard times, health problems, and having her heart broken again and again. Over time her difficult and painful experiences have transformed into lessons learned, bittersweet memories, and powerful songs that will stand the test of time.

Underneath the veneer of her tremendous success, the award-winning recording artist is a homebody who loves the simple things in life. Adele looks forward to putting down roots, starting a family, and being out of the spotlight for a while. For now, she says, she just wants to "be in love and be happy."[110]

Chapter 1: A Gifted Child

1. Quoted in Barbara Davies. "I Can't Listen to My Daughter Sing—It Reminds Me How Badly I Let Her Down: Adele's Father Reveals Torment over Their Rift." *Daily Mail* (London), February 17, 2012. www.dailymail.co.uk/femail/article-2102887/Adeles-father-reveals-torment-rift.html.

2. Quoted in Grant Rollings and Nic North. "I Was an Alcoholic and Rotten Dad to Adele. It Tears Me Up Inside." *Sun* (London), March 16, 2011. www.thesun.co.uk/sol/homepage/showbiz/bizarre/3470417/Adeles-dad-I-was-an-alcoholic-and-rotten-father.html.

3. Quoted in Jonathan Van Meter. "Adele: One and Only." *Vogue*, March 2012. www.vogue.com/magazine/article/adele-one-and-only/#1.

4. Quoted in Stuart Husband. "Adele: Young Soul Rebel." *Telegraph* (London), April 27, 2008. www.telegraph.co.uk/culture/music/3672957/Adele-young-soul-rebel.html.

5. Quoted in Sylvia Patterson. "Mad About the Girl." *Guardian* (London), January 26, 2008. www.guardian.co.uk/music/2008/jan/27/popandrock.britawards2008.

6. Quoted in Husband. "Adele."

7. Quoted in Van Meter. "Adele."

8. Quoted in Davies. "I Can't Listen to My Daughter Sing—It Reminds Me How Badly I Let Her Down."

9. Quoted in Marie Walker. "Adele: I Love the Spice Girls!" *NOW*, March 2, 2011. www.nowmagazine.co.uk/celebrity-news/517690/adele-i-love-the-spice-girls/1.

10. Quoted in Rollings and North. "I Was an Alcoholic and Rotten Dad to Adele."

11. Quoted in Touré. "Adele Opens Up About Her Inspirations, Looks and Stage Fright." *Rolling Stone*, April 28, 2011. www.rollingstone.com/music/news/adele-opens-up-about-her-inspirations-looks-and-stage-fright-20120210.

12. Quoted in Rollings and North. "I Was an Alcoholic and Rotten Dad to Adele."

13. Quoted in Davies. "I Can't Listen to My Daughter Sing—It Reminds Me How Badly I Let Her Down."

14. Quoted in Rollings and North. "I Was an Alcoholic and Rotten Dad to Adele."

15. Quoted in Van Meter. "Adele."

16. Quoted in Thelma Adams. "February Survival Guide: It's Colder than Ever and Depressingly Dark Out, and Cabin Fever Just Sets In. In the Final Stretch of Winter, *MC* Breaks Down a Pop-Culture Plan to Keep Your Spirits Up til Spring." *Marie Claire*, February 2011, p. 113.

17. Quoted in Patterson. "Mad About the Girl."

18. Quoted in Husband. "Adele."

19. Quoted in Hamish Bowles. "Feeling Groovy." *Vogue*, April 2009, p. 198.

Chapter 2: Discovered!

20. Quoted in Touré. "Adele Opens Up About Her Inspirations, Looks and Stage Fright."

21. Quoted in Bowles. "Feeling Groovy," p. 198.

22. Quoted in MTV UK. "Adele Would've Been a Teen Mum Without Brit School." March 7, 2011. www.mtv.co.uk/news/adele/261242-adele-would-ve-been-a-teen-mum-without-brit-school.

23. Quoted in Touré. "Adele Opens Up About Her Inspirations, Looks and Stage Fright."

24. Quoted in Touré. "Adele Opens Up About Her Inspirations, Looks and Stage Fright."

25. Quoted in Roy Trakin. "A Portrait of the Artist as a Fresh-Faced Ingenue, as HITS' Own Roy Trakin Interviews Her Before the Release of *19*." Adele. www.adele.tv/forum/viewtopic.php?f=2&t=20685&p=60502&hilit=songs+myspace+demo#p60502.

26. Quoted in Touré. "Adele Opens Up About Her Inspirations, Looks and Stage Fright."

27. Quoted in *Spinner* (blog), AOL Music. "Adele Recalls Hearing Pink Performing Live." December 23, 2010. www.spinner.com/2010/12/23/adele-defining-moments.

28. Quoted in Bowles. "Feeling Groovy," p. 198.

29. Quoted in Husband. "Adele."

30. Quoted in *Contactmusic.com*. "Adele's Jam Sessions with Shoniwa." August 22, 2011. www.contactmusic.com/news/adeles-jam-sessions-with-shoniwa_1241396.

31. Quoted in Trakin. "A Portrait of the Artist as a Fresh-Faced Ingenue, as HITS' Own Roy Trakin Interviews Her Before the Release of *19*."

32. Quoted in Trakin. "A Portrait of the Artist as a Fresh-Faced Ingenue, as HITS' Own Roy Trakin Interviews Her Before the Release of *19*."

33. Quoted in Pacemaker Recordings. "Latest News." October 22, 2006. http://pacemakerrecordings.com.

34. Quoted in Trakin. "A Portrait of the Artist as a Fresh-Faced Ingenue, as HITS' Own Roy Trakin Interviews Her Before the Release of *19*."

35. Quoted in Patterson. "Mad About the Girl."

36. Quoted in Kim Dawson. "Adele's Bi Guy." *Daily Star* (London). March 24, 2008. www.dailystar.co.uk/posts/view/33091.

37. Quoted in Touré. "Adele Opens Up About Her Inspirations, Looks and Stage Fright."

38. Quoted in Bethany Heitman. "Someone Like Adele: She's Famous for Heart-Wrenching Ballads—They Really Are Based on Her Painful Romantic Past (Get All the Details Here)—but This Soulful Singer Wants You to Know: She's Far Happier than Her Songs Let On." *Cosmopolitan*, December 2011, p. 38.

39. Quoted in Heitman. "Someone Like Adele," p. 38.

40. Quoted in Heitman. "Someone Like Adele," p. 38.

Chapter 3: The Making of a Star

41. Quoted in Kimbel Bouwman. "Interview with Jonathan Dickins, Manager for Adele, Jamie T, Jack Peñate." *HitQuarters*, July 14, 2008. www.hitquarters.com/index

.php3?page=intrview/opar/intrview_Jonathan_Dickins_
Interview.html.

42. Quoted in Trakin. "A Portrait of the Artist as a Fresh-Faced
    Ingenue, as HITS' Own Roy Trakin Interviews Her Before
    the Release of *19*."
43. Quoted in Bowles. "Feeling Groovy," p. 198.
44. Quoted in Bowles. "Feeling Groovy," p. 198.
45. Quoted in Heitman. "Someone Like Adele," p. 38.
46. Quoted in Trakin. "A Portrait of the Artist as a Fresh-Faced
    Ingenue, as HITS' Own Roy Trakin Interviews Her Before
    the Release of *19*."
47. Quoted in Patterson. "Mad About the Girl."
48. Quoted in Patterson. "Mad About the Girl."
49. Quoted in Trakin. "A Portrait of the Artist as a Fresh-Faced
    Ingenue, as HITS' Own Roy Trakin Interviews Her Before
    the Release of *19*."
50. Caspar Llewellyn Smith. "CD: Adele, *19*." *Guardian*
    (London), January 2008.
51. Michael Menachem. "Adele: Chasing Pavements." *Billboard*,
    June 7, 2008, p. 50.
52. Chuck Arnold. "Adele." *People*, June 23, 2008, p. 44.
53. Quoted in Bouwman. "Interview with Jonathan Dickins,
    Manager for Adele, Jamie T, Jack Peñate."

Chapter 4: More Heartbreak, More Hits

54. Quoted in *Heat*. "Alex Sturrock Is the Boyfriend That
    Inspired Adele's Sad Songs." April 3, 2012. www.heatworld
    .com/Celeb-News/2012/03/Alex-Sturrock-is-the-boyfriend-
    that-inspired-Adeles-sad-songs.
55. Quoted in Anderson Cooper. "The Year of Adele." Video.
    60 Minutes, CBS News, February 12, 2012. www.cbsnews.
    com/video/watch/?id=7398480n&tag=contentBody;
    storyMediaBox.
56. Quoted in Trakin. "A Portrait of the Artist as a Fresh-Faced
    Ingenue, as HITS' Own Roy Trakin Interviews Her Before
    the Release of *19*."

57. Quoted in *Heat*. "Alex Sturrock Is the Boyfriend That Inspired Adele's Sad Songs."

58. Quoted in Trakin. "A Portrait of the Artist as a Fresh-Faced Ingenue, as HITS' Own Roy Trakin Interviews Her Before the Release of *19*."

59. Quoted in Bouwman. "Interview with Jonathan Dickins, Manager for Adele, Jamie T, Jack Peñate."

60. Quoted in *Contactmusic.com*. "Adele Explains 2008 Booze & Love Meltdown." June 8, 2009. www.contactmusic.com/news/adele-explains-2008-booze-love-meltdown_1105845.

61. Quoted in *Contactmusic.com*. "Adele Credits Palin with U.S. Success." January 12, 2011. www.contactmusic.com/news/adele-credits-palin-with-us-success_1194863.

62. Quoted in Bowles. "Feeling Groovy," p. 198.

63. Quoted in Bowles. "Feeling Groovy," p. 198.

64. Quoted in Bowles. "Feeling Groovy," p. 198.

65. Quoted in Touré. "Adele Opens Up About Her Inspirations, Looks and Stage Fright."

66. Quoted in Van Meter. "Adele."

67. Quoted in Adele. "*21* Track by Track Interview." Video ("Rolling in the Deep"). www.adele.tv/trackbytrack/archive.

68. Quoted in Cooper. "The Year of Adele."

69. Quoted in Adele. "*21* Track by Track Interview."

70. Quoted in Adele. "*21* Track by Track Interview."

71. Quoted in Adele. "*21* Track by Track Interview."

72. Camille Paglia. "The True Voice of America—Adele from Tottenham: The Singer Swept All Before Her at the Grammys." *Sunday Times* (London), February 19, 2012, p. 3.

73. Edna Gundersen. "Adele Had a Very Good Year." *USA Today*, December 27, 2011, p. 01D.

74. Quoted in Edna Gundersen. "Adele's Deeply Personal Style Rolls On." *USA Today*, February 9, 2012, p. 01D.

75. Patterson. "Mad About the Girl."

76. Jim Farber. "Adele '21' Review: Perfect Album Floats Beyond Countries and Time." *New York Daily News*, February 22,

2011. www.nydailynews.com/entertainment/music-arts/
adele-21-review-perfect-album-floats-countries-time-
article-1.135557#ixzz1x3xFrxqA.

77. Quoted in Van Meter. "Adele."
78. Beth Teitell. "Why Cry over 'Someone'?" *Boston Globe*,
February 7, 2012. www.boston.com/ae/music/articles/
2012/02/07/why_does_adeles_grammy_nominated_
someone_like_you_make_people_cry/?page=2.
79. Quoted in Teitell. "Why Cry over 'Someone'?"
80. Quoted in Teitell. "Why Cry over 'Someone'?"
81. Quoted in Cooper. "The Year of Adele."
82. Van Meter. "Adele."
83. Quoted in Cooper. "The Year of Adele."
84. Quoted in Van Meter. "Adele."

Chapter 5: Career Crisis

85. Quoted in Cooper. "The Year of Adele."
86. Quoted in Cooper. "The Year of Adele."
87. Jon Caramanica, Jon Pareles, and Nate Chinen. "Critics
Choice: New CDs." *New York Times*, February 28, 2011. www
.nytimes.com/2011/03/01/arts/music/01choice.html?_r=1.
88. Farber. "Adele '21' Review."
89. Quoted in Van Meter. "Adele."
90. Quoted in Cooper. "The Year of Adele."
91. Quoted in Van Meter. "Adele."
92. Quoted in Edna Gundersen. "Grammys Will Be Adele's
Vocal 'Debut.'" *USA Today*, February 10, 2012, p. 02D.
93. Quoted in Cooper. "The Year of Adele."
94. Quoted in *54th Annual Grammy Awards*. CBS, February 12,
2012.
95. Quoted in *54th Annual Grammy Awards*.
96. Sally Biddulph. "Adele Stars at the Grammys." Seven News
(Australia). Yahoo! 7 News, February 13, 2012. http://
au.news.yahoo.com/video/national/watch/28285391/adele-
stars-at-grammys/.

Chapter 6: Getting Real with Adele

97. Quoted in Van Meter. "Adele."
98. Van Meter. "Adele."
99. Van Meter. "Adele."
100. Quoted in Adams. "February Survival Guide," p. 113.
101. Quoted in Charlotte Cowles. "Karl Lagerfeld Calls Adele Fat, Loves the Obamas, and Says Something Weird About Pregnant Women." *New York Magazine*, February 6, 2012. http://nymag.com/daily/fashion/2012/02/karl-lagerfeld-calls-adele-fat-loves-the-obamas.html.
102. Quoted in Robert Erdmann and James Patrick Herman. "I Don't Care About Being a Size." *Glamour*, December 2008, p. 270.
103. Quoted in Cooper. "The Year of Adele."
104. Quoted in Liz Jones. "Adele: 'I Have All the Say; I Have Power over Everything I Do.'" *Daily Mail* (London), February 13, 2009. www.dailymail.co.uk/home/you/article-1135182/Adele-I-say-I-power-I-do.html.
105. Quoted in Van Meter. "Adele."
106. Quoted in Van Meter. "Adele."
107. Quoted in Davies. "I Can't Listen to My Daughter Sing—It Reminds Me How Badly I Let Her Down."
108. Quoted in Cooper. "The Year of Adele."
109. Adele Adkins. "I've Got Some News." Adele blog, June 29, 2012. www.adele.tv/blog.
110. Quoted in Van Meter. "Adele."

Important Dates

1988

Adele Laurie Blue Adkins is born on May 5 in Tottenham, North London, England.

1991

Adele's father moves to Wales.

1998

Moves with her mom to Brixton, South London; later they move to West Norwood, South London.

2002

Is profoundly influenced by the music of Ella Fitzgerald and Etta James.

2003

Enrolls at age fifteen in the BRIT School, a performing arts school in Croydon, London.

2004

Writes "Hometown Glory."

2006

Graduates from the BRIT School; hires a business manager and signs with indie record company XL Recordings; gives her first public appearance, opening for singer Jack Peñate at the Troubadour in London.

2007

After a breakup, writes the songs for her first album; her first single record, "Hometown Glory," is released in the UK.

2008

Her debut album, *19*, is released in Europe; receives the Critics Choice award (for most promising artist) at the Brit Awards; begins her first record tour; makes a record deal between Columbia Records in the United States and XL Recordings; makes her U.S. debut at Joe's Pub in New York; *19* is released in the United States; quits her concert tour to be with her boyfriend; revives her career by performing on *Saturday Night Live*; is nominated for four Grammy Awards; wins the BBC annual end-of-year "Sound Of" poll.

2009

Wins two Grammys, for Best New Artist and Best Female Pop Vocal Performance (for "Chasing Pavements"); appears as herself on the TV show *Ugly Betty*; breaks up with her boyfriend; spends the next year working on a new album.

2010

"Rolling in the Deep" is released—a preview to her second album.

2011

Second album, *21*, is released; begins her second world tour; after recurring voice problems, a polyp on her vocal cords hemorrhages; is forced to cancel several concerts and undergoes surgery to remove the polyp on her vocal cords; does not speak or sing for over two months; is nominated for six Grammy Awards.

2012

The media reveals that she has a new boyfriend, Simon Konecki; wins six Grammy Awards; has baby boy on October 19.

For More Information

Books

Adele. *Adele: 19*. Milwaukee, WI: Hal Leonard, 2009. This book gives readers a behind-the-scenes look at Adele's first world tour to promote the album *19*. Includes black-and-white photos.

Katherine Krohn. *Ella Fitzgerald*. Minneapolis: Twenty-First Century Books, 2001. Adele considers Ella Fitzgerald to be one of her strongest influences as a singer. This award-winning biography looks at the life and times of the jazz legend.

DVD

Adele Live at the Royal Albert Hall. Directed by Paul Dugdale. New York: Sony, 2011. This DVD captures Adele's concert at the Royal Albert Hall. It was filmed shortly before Adele's vocal cord surgery.

Periodicals

Hamish Bowles. "Feeling Groovy." *Vogue*, April 2009.

Nicole Frehsée. "Meet Adele, the U.K.'s Newest Soul Star." *Rolling Stone*, January 22, 2009.

Edna Gundersen. "Adele's Deeply Personal Style Rolls On." *USA Today*. February 9, 2012.

Andrew Leahey. "Live at the Royal Albert Hall." *Washington Times*, November 29, 2011.

Caspar Llewellyn Smith. "CD: Adele, *19*." *Guardian* (London), January 2008.

Internet Sources

Adele. "*21* Track by Track Interview." www.adele.tv/trackbytrack/archive.

Kimbel Bouwman. "Interview with Jonathan Dickins, Manager for Adele, Jamie T, Jack Peñate." *HitQuarters*, July 14, 2008. www.hitquarters.com/index.php3?page=intrview/opar/intrview_Jonathan_Dickins_Interview.html.

Stuart Husband. "Adele: Young Soul Rebel." *Telegraph* (London), April 27, 2008. www.telegraph.co.uk/culture/music/3672957/Adele-young-soul-rebel.html.

Sylvia Patterson. "Mad About the Girl." *Guardian* (London). January 26, 2008. www.guardian.co.uk/music/2008/jan/27/popandrock.britawards2008.

Touré. "Adele Opens Up About Her Inspirations, Looks and Stage Fright." *Rolling Stone*, April 28, 2011. www.rollingstone.com/music/news/adele-opens-up-about-her-inspirations-looks-and-stage-fright-20120210.

Jonathan Van Meter. "Adele: One and Only." *Vogue*, March 2012. www.vogue.com/magazine/article/adele-one-and-only/#1.

Websites

Adele (www.adele.tv/home). Adele's official website includes her blog, forum, photos, news, and other information.

"Adele," People.com (http://www.people.com/people/adele). This site has biographical information as well as fun facts, current news, photos, and videos of the singer.

A

Accent, 8

Adele Live (second world tour), 65, 65–66, 67–68

Adkins, Anita (aunt), 13

Adkins, Kim (aunt), 13

Adkins, Penny (mother), 12, 13, 18, 21, 31, 53, 84

Awards and honors
2009 Grammy, 53, 54
2012 Grammy, 8, 72–74, 74, 76–77, 77, 83
Billboard's Hot 100 chart, 61–62, 64
Brit Awards Critics Choice Award, 52, 75, 75
number one breakthrough act of 2008, 52–53
"Sound Of" poll (BBC), 53
United Kingdom number one single, 61, 64

B

"Best for Last" (song), 42

Beyoncé, 19, 20, 88

Billboard's Hot 100 chart, 61–62, 64

Birth, 12

Björk, 39, 40

Blues music, 12, 13

Brit Awards Critics Choice Award, 52, 75, 75

BRIT (British Record Industry Trust) School for Performing Arts and Technology, 9, 22–26, 24, 32–33

British Broadcasting Company (BBC), 53

C

"Chasing Pavements" (song), 41

Childhood
homes, 9, 14, 18
importance of extended family, 13, 16
music during, 12, 13–16, 15, 18, 19, 20, 21
relationship of parents, 12
shows put on, 16
style, 19, 20, 21

Clothing
2009 Grammy Awards, 53, 54
2012 Grammy Awards, 74, 83
daily, 53, 80–81, 81

"Cold Shoulder" (song), 40

D

"Daydreamer" (song), 32, 38, 40

"Delly from the Block," 14

"Delly-cat," 20

Dickins, Jonathan, 35–36, 37–38, 45

Drinking, 11, 36, 49, 51, 67

Drugs, using, 36

E

Education
behavior at local school, 21
BRIT School, 9, 22–26, 24, 32–33
moves and, 18

Epworth, Paul, 60–61
Evans, Cameron (half brother), 18, 86
Evans, John (grandfather), 17, 18–19
Evans, Mark (father), 12, 16–18, 19, 84–86, 85
Evans, Rose (grandmother), 17, 86
An Evening with Adele (first world tour), 48
    preparations, 46
    return to, 54, 57
    Sturrock, 47, 49–51
    success, 49, 50

F
Fame, realities of, 41
Fey, Tina, 51
Fitzgerald, Ella, 27, 29
Flack, Roberta, 29

G
Gabrielle, 15, 16, 19
Grammy Awards
    2009, 53, 54
    2012, 8, 72–74, 74, 76–77, 77, 83
    James, Etta, 28

H
Health, 66, 67–68, 69–70
Hobbies, 80
Home, 86–87
"Hometown Glory" (song)
    on demo, 35
    first public performance, 38
    as first release, 37
    writing, 31–32
Huggett, Nick, 33–34, 37, 60

I
Island Records, 32

J
James, Etta, 28, 28, 29
Jamie T, 35, 42

K
Konecki, Simon, 70, 70–72, 80, 87–88

L
Lagerfeld, Karl, 82
Laryngitis, 66, 67–68
Later... with Jools Holland (television program), 15–16, 38–40
Louis Armstrong (pet miniature dachshund), 70, 80

M
Madonna, 88
McCartney, Paul, 39, 40, 76
"Melt My Heart to Stone" (song), 42
Music
    BRIT School, 9, 22–26, 24, 32–33
    during childhood, 14–16, 18, 19, 20, 21
    influence of parents, 12, 13–14, 61
    influence of performers, 26–29, 27, 28
    inspirations for songs, 32, 40–42, 58, 60
    lack of vocal training, 21, 24, 29
    lessons, 9, 21
    reviews from critics, 44–45, 50, 61, 62–64, 66–67
    See also 19 (album); *21* (album); *specific songs*

Music industry
  BRIT and, 23, 25
  first contact with, 32–34
  first performance, 37–38
  work in record store, 55
  XL Recordings, 32–34, 42
"My Same" (song), 68
MySpace, discovery on, 9, 32

N
Name
  given by parents, 12, 13
  nicknames, 14, 20
  professional, 36–37
Nan, 13
19 (album), 44
  inspiration for, 86
  naming, 66
  reviews, 44–45, 50
  sales, 52, 55
  sales after 2012 Grammys, 77
Noisettes, 25, 30, 30

P
Pacemaker Recordings, 42
Palin, Sarah, 52
Paltrow, Gwyenth, 73
Peñate, Jack, 37–38
Pet, 70, 80
Photographer, official, 47, 50, 53
Pink concert, 26–27
Pregnancy, 87–88

R
Rock music, 13–14
"Rolling in the Deep" (song), 58, 60, 61, 64, 73
Romantic relationships
  eHarmony, 71
  Konecki, Simon, 70, 70–72, 80, 87–88

Sturrock, Alex, 46–47, 49–51, 53–55, 57–58, 60
Royal Albert Hall
  performance, 68
Russell, Richard, 34, 35

S
Saturday Night Live (television program), 51–52, 52, 63
Shoniwa, Shingai, 25, 30, 30
Smith, Dan, 25, 30, 30
Smoking, 11, 36, 49, 67
"Someone Like You" (song), 58, 60, 61–64
Spice Girls, 17, 18
Stage fright, 11, 38–40, 49
Sturrock, Alex
  breakup, 55
  engagement to another, 57–58, 60
  Grammy Awards, 53
  identity kept from media, 46
  as photographer, 46–47, 49–51
  relationship problems, 53–54
Sylvia Young Theatre School, 21–22

T
Television
  appearances on American, 51–52, 52, 57
  appearances on British, 38–40
  influence of, during childhood, 14–16
  song spoofed on Saturday Night Live, 63
  songs featured on, 31
Thomas, Ben, 26

Tours
  Adele Live (second world), *65*,
    65–66, 67–68
  An Evening with Adele (first
    world), 46, 47, *48*, 49–51,
    54, 57
Troubadour, 38
21 (album), 67
  inspiration for, 58, 86
  naming, 66
  reviews, 66–67
  sales, 62, 77

U
Ugly Betty (television program),
    57
United States
  An Evening with Adele tour, 50,
    51, 54
  television appearances, 51–52,
    52, 57

V
Vacations, 82
Voice
  acute laryngitis, 66, 67–68
  after surgery, 73
  lack of training, 21, 24, 29
  opinion of critics, 45
  polyp on vocal chords, 69
  range, 29

W
Wales, 12, 16–18
Weight, 82, 84
Winehouse, Amy, 29, 36, *36*

X
XL Recordings, 32–34, 42
  See also 19 (album); *21* (album)

Z
Zeitels, Steven, 69, 73

Picture Credits

Cover © Adrian Sanchez-Gonzalez/ZUMA Press/Corbis
© adrian lourie/Alamy, 33, 43
© Ann Summa/Liaison/Getty Images, 17
© AP Images/Chris Pizzello, 79
© AP Images/Mark J. Terrill, 77
© AP Images/Matt Sayles, 74
© CBS via Getty Images, 87
© Daily Mail/Rex/Alamy, 24
© Dana Edelson/NBC/NBCU Photo Bank via Getty Images, 52
© Dave Etheridge-Barnes/Getty Images, 39
© Dave J. Hogan/Getty Images, 10, 75
© Dimitrios Kambouris/WireImage/Getty Images, 59
© Gilles Petard/Redferns/Getty Images, 27
© James Davies/Alamy, 85
© Jason Kirk/Newsmakers/Getty Images, 20
© Jeff Kravitz/FilmMagic/Getty Images, 36
© Jo Hale/Getty Images, 30
© John Shearer/WireImage/Getty Images, 54
© Katy Raddatz/San Francisco Chronicle/Corbis, 37
© Kevin Mazur/WireImage/Getty Images, 62, 70
© Lenscap/Alamy, 44
© Michael Ochs Archives/Getty Images, 28
© Neil Mockford/FilmMagic/Getty Images, 81
© Paul Bergen/Redferns/Getty Images, 14, 43, 48
© Ray Tamarra/Getty Images, 56
© Stefan M. Prager/Redferns/Getty Images, 65
© Steve Granitz/WireImage/Getty Images, 83
© Studio 101/Alamy, 67
© UK History/Alamy, 15

About the Author

Katherine Krohn is the author of many books, including biographies of musicians Shakira, Michael Jackson, Gwen Stefani, and Elvis Presley. Krohn received a Carter G. Woodson award for her biography of legendary jazz singer Ella Fitzgerald. For more information about Krohn and her books, you can visit her website at http://katherinekrohn.com.